# Rolling Stock Revival

By

Winston Guy

## Trademark Disclaimer

All trademarks, logos and brand names are the property of their respective owners. All company, product and service names used in this book are for identification purposes only. Use of these names, trademarks and brands does not imply endorsement.

# Contents

# Introduction

I have spent a number of years painting and weathering model railway items of various types from locomotives and rolling stock to buildings to bring an element of realism to standard models. These models have found homes worldwide and, I am sure, brought enjoyment to their new owners.

I would not deem myself an expert on the subject and I am not somebody who believes themselves to be a "pro-weatherer" whatever that means. This is my hobby, I enjoy it and my results fall, happily, between those of the true weathering artists with price tags to match and those that seem to bear little resemblance to anything in the real world.

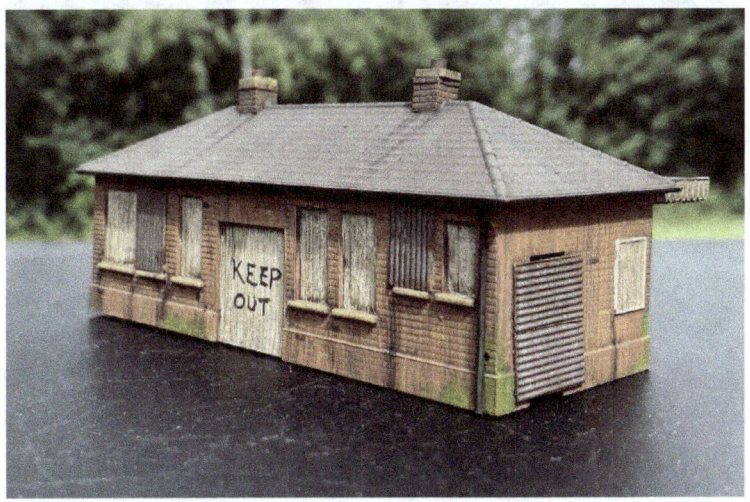

However, the thing that I enjoy most is bringing that element of realism to a model that would otherwise be firmly regarded as a toy. Whether that be low price modern models or rather elderly railway rolling stock, the same basic premise applies; shiny, unrealistic plastic finish on an otherwise perfectly acceptable model that can be elevated in appearance with some careful painting and weathering.

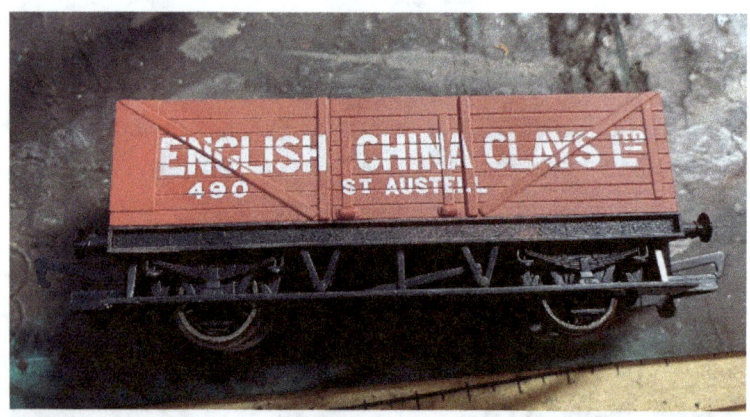

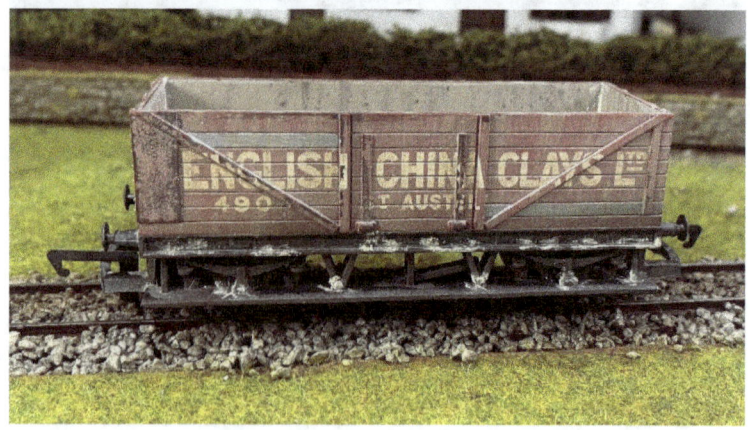

In the current financial climate, the option of reusing an existing item at a fraction of the cost of a new item would seem to tick financial and environmental boxes. Why spend

£20 or £30 on a new item when an existing item can be bought for £3 and diverted from landfill?

As always, there has to be a compromise, which in this case comes in the form of detail. A modern model from modern tooling will, usually, be vastly more detailed than a 1970s model but do you really need that amount of detail on a working layout? Can it actually be seen from a normal viewing distance? Will it just get broken off anyway? At the end of the day, detail costs money so how much do you want to spend?

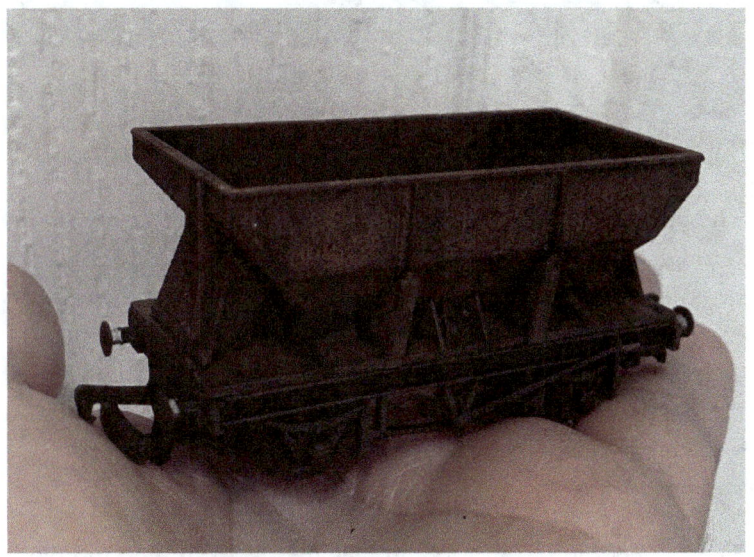

In this book, I will show how you can easily paint and weather some of the most common OO wagons of the 1960s to 1980s to look acceptable on a modern layout.

This book is not about super detailing models or achieving "exhibition standard" weathering on already good models, there are plenty of books on those areas already.

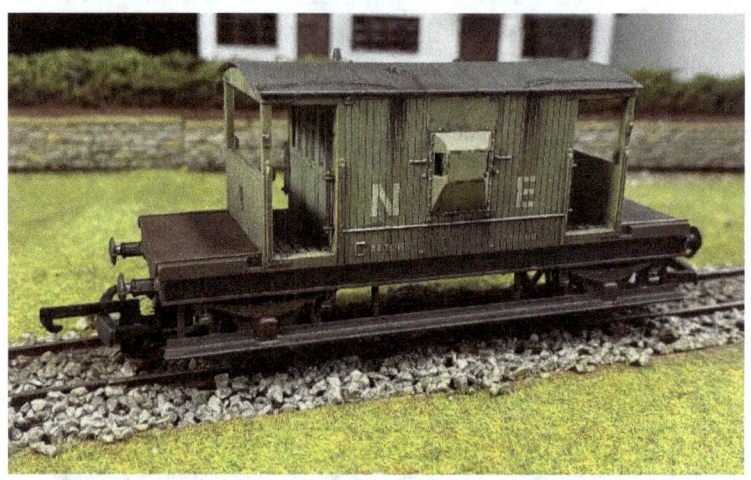

The projects in this book are ordered to gradually take you through an increasing number of painting and weathering techniques in each project, building on the techniques from each previous project to develop your skill set. Even if you decide that the projects become too ambitious for you to feel comfortable with, just having the skills from the first project will stand you in good stead to make a difference to your rolling stock.

The subject models in each project are just examples and the techniques are equally applicable to other similar items so, for example, the techniques for addressing a Triang plank wagon can also be applied to shiny red Triang brick wagons.

Throughout your journey into weathering, it is worth remembering that this is mainly a painting process. Hence, it needs to be considered more as an art form rather than a science, there is no one right way to do things and the result somebody else wants may not be the result you want.

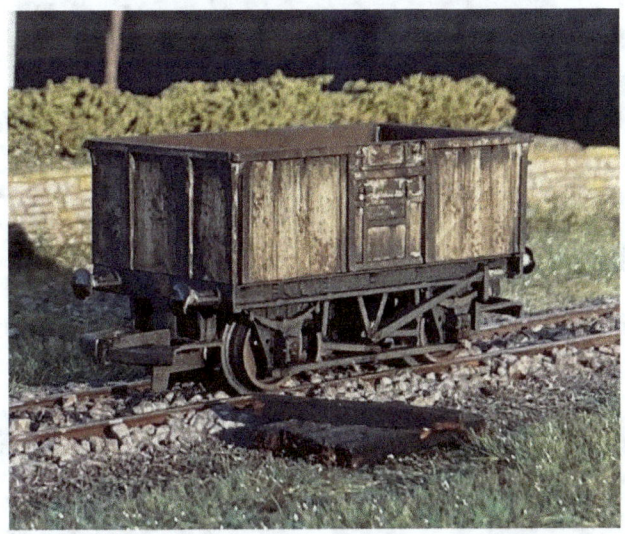

There are a multitude of ways to weather railway models, this book just sets out the way I go about things. If you go by another route and get the result you want, then that is another way to do it.

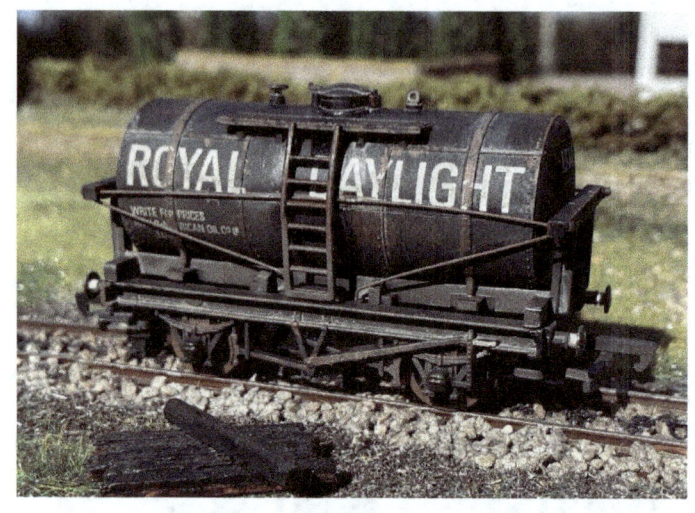

Be brave and experiment once you have got the hang of the basics, if an idea works then it was not stupid!

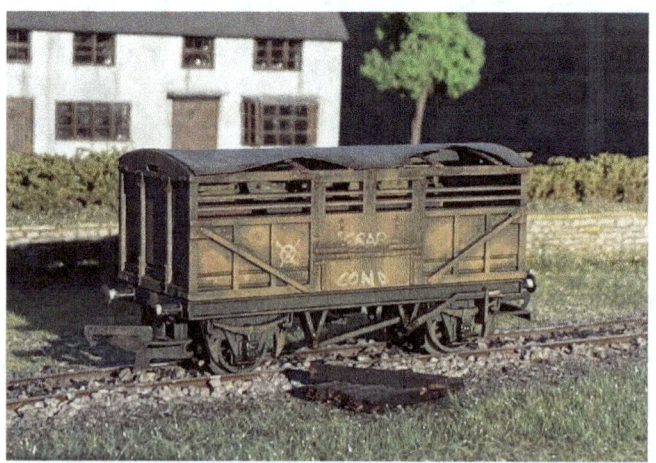

# Chapter 1 – The Basics

The following points are some basics to make life easier in your endeavours when sourcing and working on your elderly models.

- Avoid badly damaged items unless you have a stash of spare chasses and the like – buying spare parts is costly and can negate the cost advantage of using old models.
- Avoid metal chassis Triang items (unless you have a plastic chassis to fit) – the metal chassis wagons are not easily upgraded to modern metal wheels and often feature early style tension lock couplings.
- Avoid Hornby Dublo items – the couplings on these items are not compatible with modern tension lock couplings so are best avoided.
- Be careful with early Lima items which are HO masquerading as OO – these items can be noticeably out of scale and are often continental outline items rebadged for the UK market.
- Upgrade to metal wheels – modern metal wheel sets provide far better running than 1970s or 1980s plastic wheel sets.
- Triang & Hornby plastic chassis models were made in standard sizes so bodies can be swapped from one chassis to another of the same size (e.g., plank wagons, vent vans and small tank wagons mostly use the same chassis). This is handy for combining parts from multiple damaged wagons if the need arises.

- The techniques for dealing with old rolling stock can be equally as effective in elevating some modern "budget" items like wagons from the Hornby "Railroad" range.

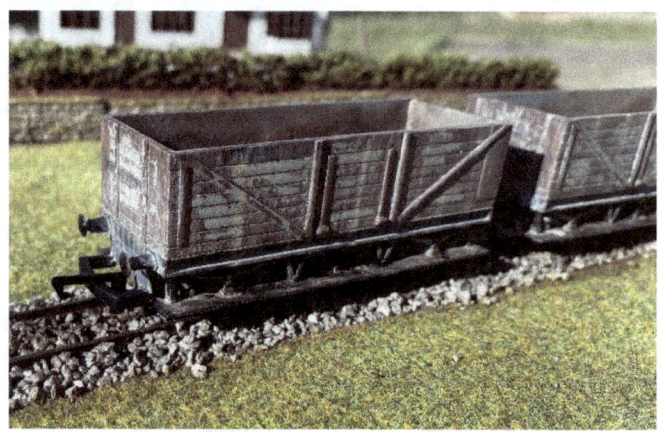

- Take your time! Yes, there are YouTube videos of wagons being weathered in 15 minutes and the projects outlined in this book can take up to 10 days with drying time between products but will produce significantly better results than a rush job with an airbrush or some powders.

Perhaps the single most important rule is do not undertake a weathering project on anything you cannot tolerate writing off if it goes wrong! I have weathered hundreds of wagons and I still do not work on expensive items for other people, I cannot cope with the stress of something going wrong!

A lot of the products I employ in this book are enamel or oil paint based, these have the benefits of long drying times and ability to be adjusted or removed with appropriate thinners on a brush if you are not happy with how it looks. Acrylic products do not have this luxury and you need to get it right first time, so they are faster to use but at higher risk for the novice.

Start with some cheap items until you are confident you can do a more expensive item justice, hopefully this book will guide you through those first few projects.

You might find that, to make best use of time and paints, and to gain more practice, that it is worth doing each project on multiple wagons at the same time.

The results of these projects will be satisfying in themselves and will give you a good set of skills for weathering other items.

# Chapter 2 – Equipment

For each of the projects in this book, I will identify the specific equipment or materials required but a set of basic equipment will be needed to complete any of the projects.

None of these items will break the bank and most will likely be in any railway modeller's arsenal already.

- **Screwdrivers:** A set of small sized screwdrivers are useful for dealing with occasional body screws or just for carefully prising bodies and chasses apart. If you are going to be regularly taking apart rolling stock, a set of plastic tools for removing car interior plastic clips are a cheap addition and less likely to damage plastic or hands.

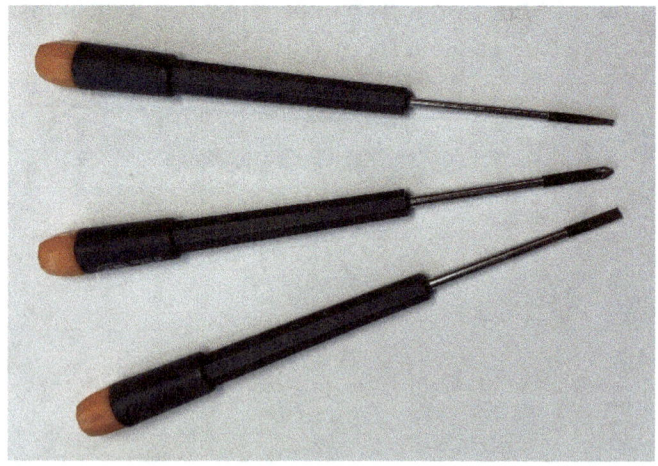

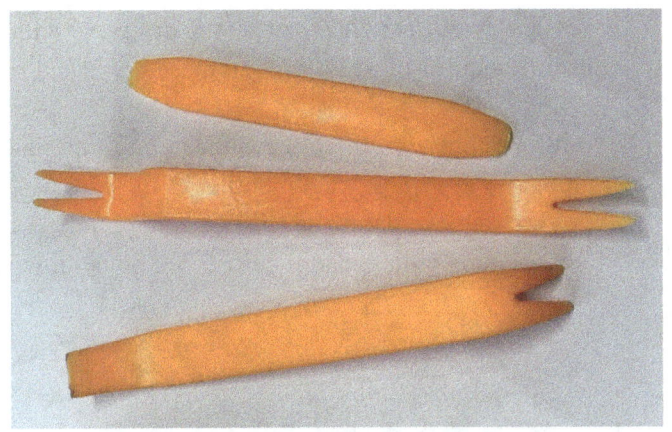

- **Modelling knife:** For the majority of these projects, a chisel type blade will be of more use than a super sharp scalpel as it will mainly be used for scaping rather than cutting.

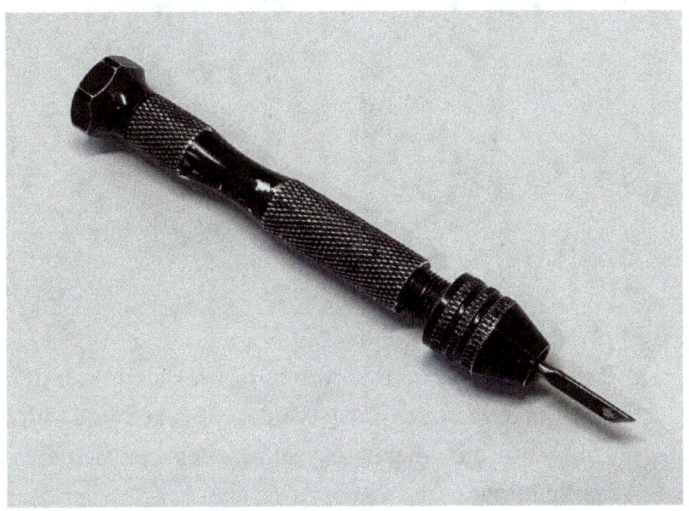

- **Wet & dry paper;** 1200 grit wet & dry paper should be sufficient for most sanding in these projects.

- **Glue:** A rubberised (black) cyanoacrylate super glue is ideal for attaching wagon bodies to the chassis if clips are loose or damaged (just be sure you do not want to remove them again before you apply glue!).

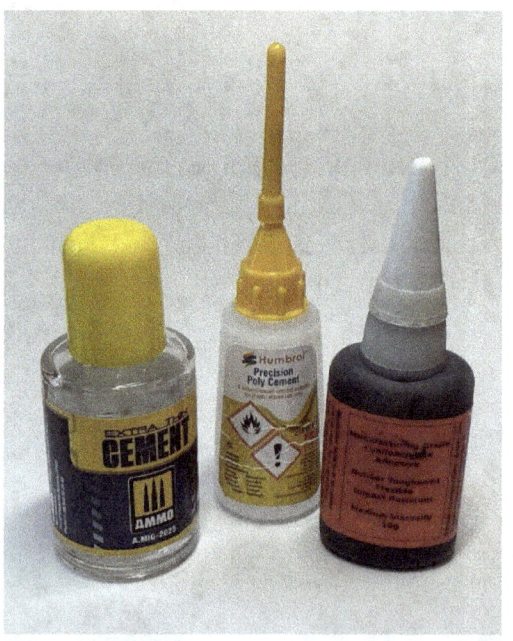

- **Paint brushes:** an assortment of brushes from 10/0 up to 12 will cover most eventualities and you will gradually find what suits you best for a particular application.

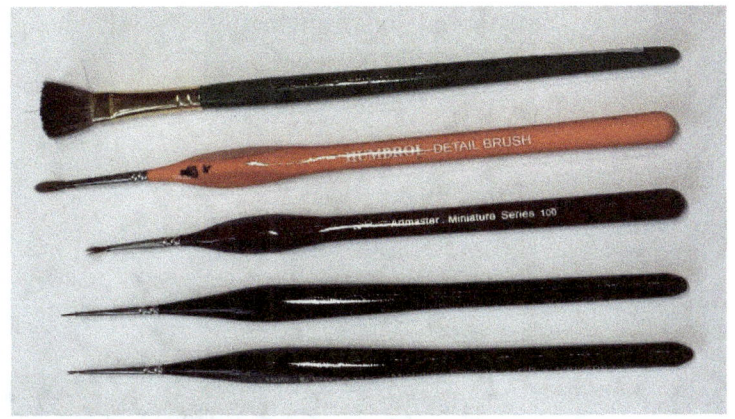

- **Sponges:** The easiest way to obtain these is to cut up
  a car washing sponge into suitable sized chunks

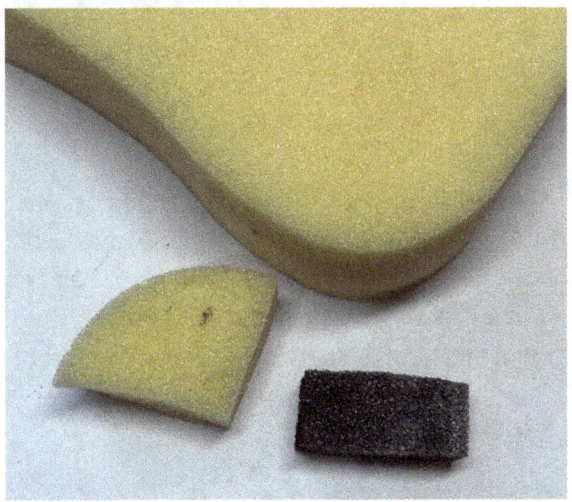

- **Palette;** Not a big wooden one but a small plastic one
  for paint! These are available in cheap sets from most
  shops with an art department, squeezing small

amounts of paint from bottles of acrylic into the palette makes life easier.

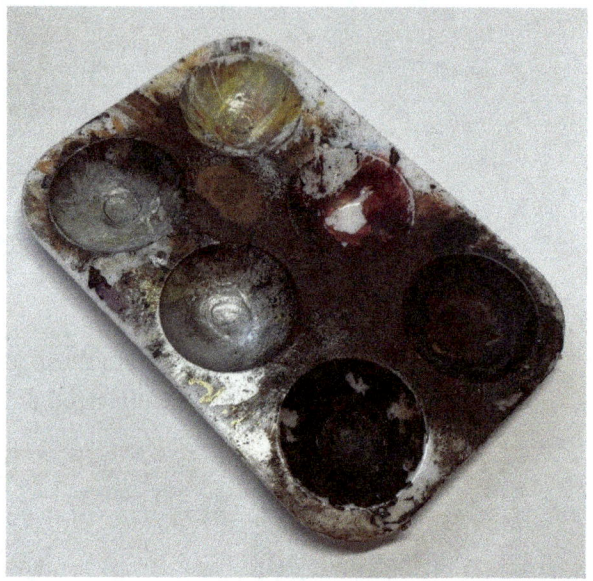

- **Airbrush:** This is a big one but need not cost a fortune. For the majority of my railway weathering, I use a £15 airbrush with a 0.3mm nozzle and needle which is perfectly adequate and a bit less finnicky about cleaning than my more expensive airbrushes.

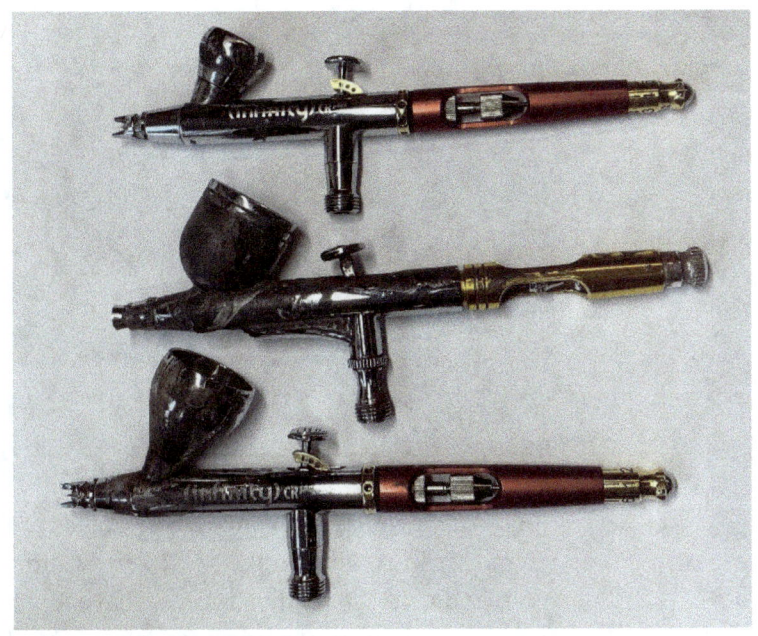

-   **Compressed Air;** To drive your airbrush. I use a small compressor as I undertake frequent airbrush work but for lesser amounts of work a canister will suffice.

-   **Airbrush cleaning tools:** A nozzle scraper, set of nozzle cleaners and set of nozzle brushes will remove built up gunk that will not shift with airbrush cleaner fluid alone.

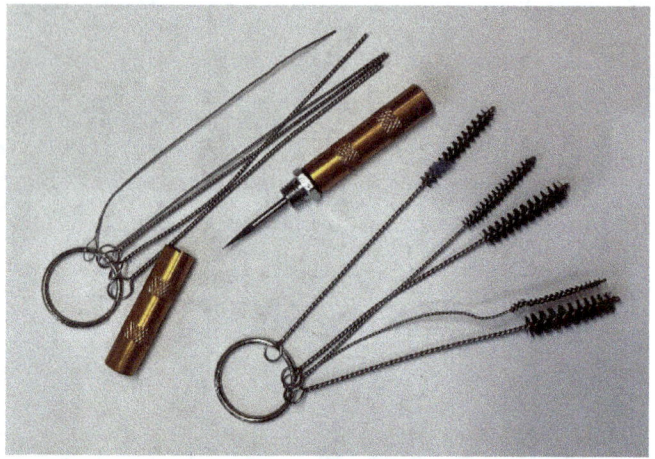

- **Somewhere to use your airbrush;** This is probably the most critical item on the list. I do my airbrush work in the garage but that means I have to deal with fluctuations in temperature and humidity. Modern acrylic paints do not have the same solvent fume issues that enamels suffered from but still produce airborne paint particles that will settle onto surfaces. Airbrush booths with fans are available but come at a cost.

- **Acrylic paints & acrylic thinners;** A selection of acrylic paints are called up in this book, appropriate thinners will be needed to ensure they spray correctly. Acrylic paints are used as they avoid the solvent fume issues of enamels, are fast drying and are resistant to the solvent in our enamel washes. Acrylic paints can be thinned with water but the alcohol content in the acrylic thinners stops the paint beading into patches which tends to happen when just water is used.

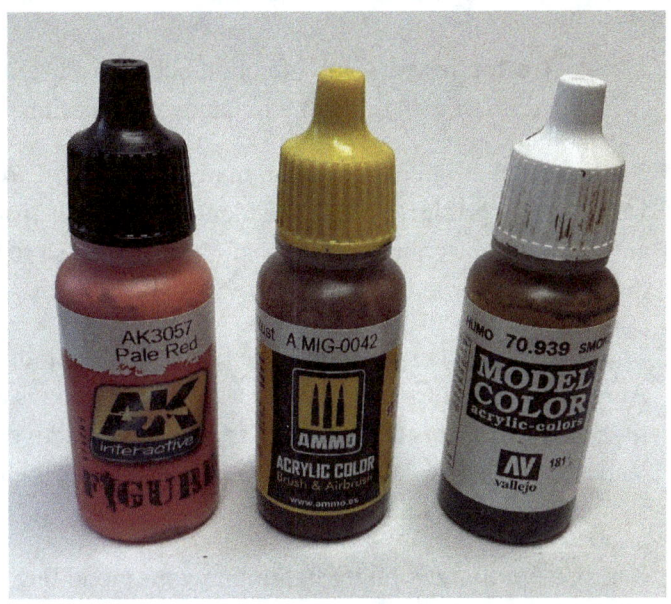

- **Odourless enamel thinners;** Used throughout these projects in conjunction with enamel and oil-based weathering products. Enamel and oil-based washes are a more forgiving option compared to acrylic products which dry rapidly and permanently. Oils or enamels allow for the effect to be manipulated, or even removed, using thinners which is very useful, especially for someone beginning their foray into weathering techniques. The odourless thinner, as the name suggests, is much more conducive to being used inside the house.

- **Paper towel:** A roll of kitchen roll or similar is going to be in constant use during these projects.

- **Cotton buds:** A tub of cotton buds are a useful addition that will come in handy on occasion.

Aside from these items, the main materials required are various paint products which are identified in each project, and most will be common across all the projects, so reducing the number of products you need.

The paint products I use tend to be from the Mig Jiminez Ammo range, but I supplement these with other items as I see fit. Similar products are available from AK Interactive, Vallejo and a number of other manufacturers, all of which should be equally suitable.

It is also worth mentioning lighting in your modelling area as too little can make it difficult to see what you are doing, and the wrong colour light can impact on your perception of the colours you apply to the model. I use a white LED desk lamp above my work area to provide a crisp, white light.

# Chapter 3 – Making a Start

So, you have now decided to have a go at the projects in this book, where do you start?

First of all, following the points given in Chapter 1, choose your victims!

The photo below shows some of the items used in this book in their as received condition.

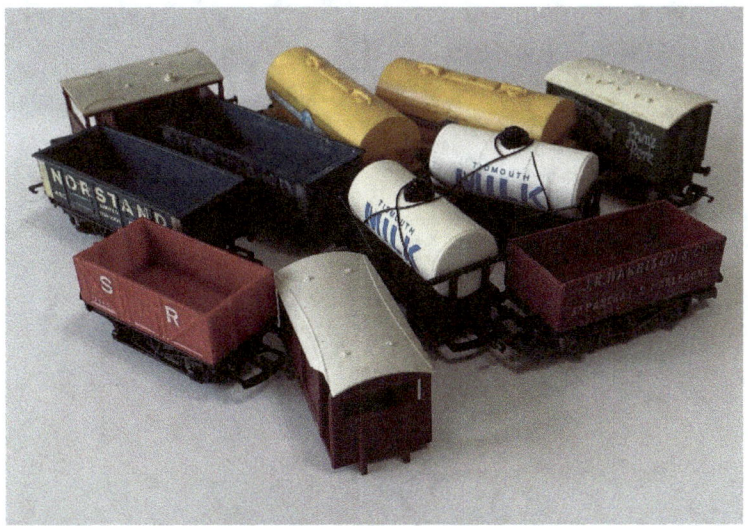

What is not immediately obvious from the photo is how disgustingly dirty the items all were. When dealing with items that have endured anything up to sixty years of handling and storage there is bound to be an accumulation of grime.

Removing this layer of grime and grease deposits is critical in order to ensure that our paint layers adhere firmly to the surface of the item.

My first port of call for most items is a simple soak in some washing-up liquid and cold water (not warm water, to avoid distorting the plastic).

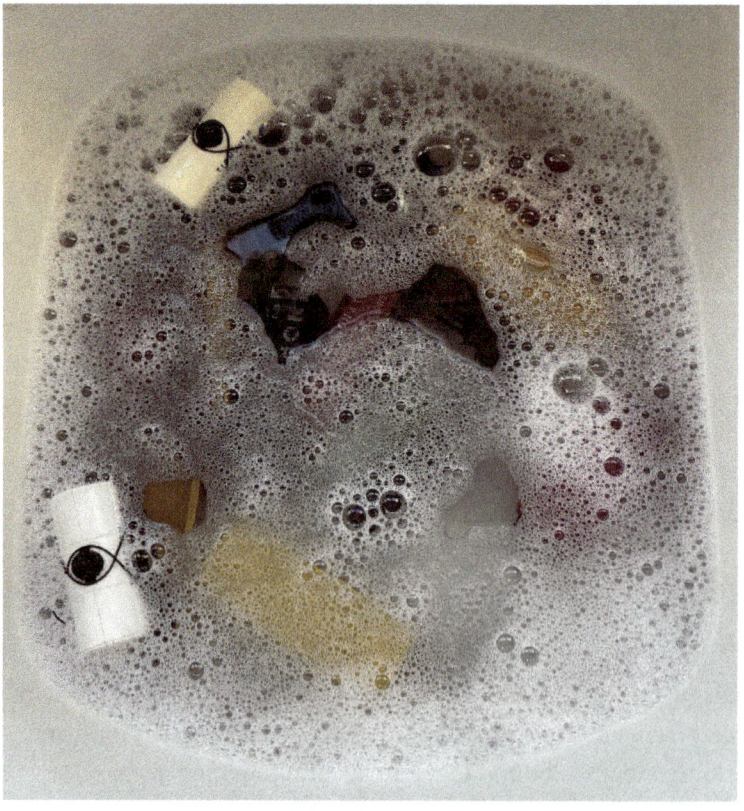

This is followed by a scrub with a dish brush, cold water rinse and air drying.

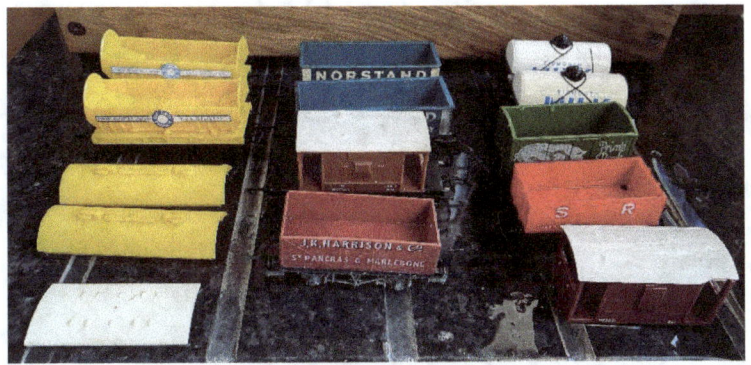

Either before or after washing, most items will require basic dismantling to allow the body, roof, and chassis to undergo separate painting processes.

Dismantling varies from wagon to wagon, depending on manufacturer and type but some basic examples are shown below using the items in the projects.

One quirk that is worth noting is that Triang and Hornby goods wagon roofs generally just lift off, but brake van roofs are usually glued in place, so do not try to remove those!

A large proportion of Hornby and Triang mineral, plank and goods wagon bodies are attached to the chassis using a post on each corner which is melted over in manufacture.

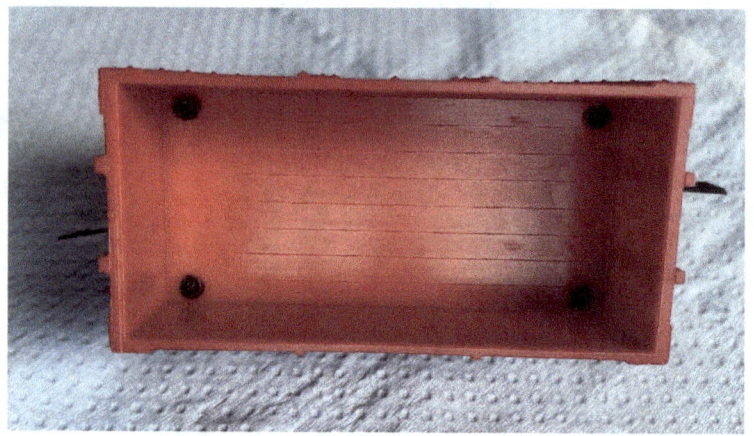

These bodies can be gently prised away from the chassis at each corner in turn.

I tend to start by using a small electrical screwdriver at one corner to get started, this can then be followed by a plastic car interior clip removal tool to minimise the risk of damage or injury.

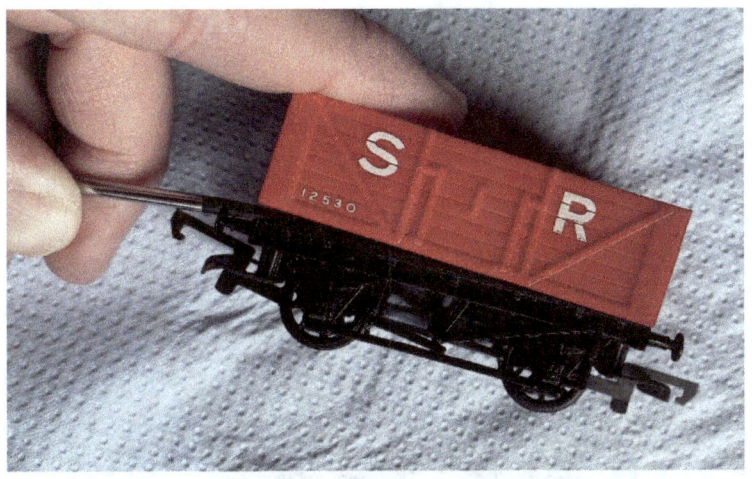

Once the posts have been prised away, you will be left with three items:

- Chassis
- Counterweight (unless chassis is metal)
- Body

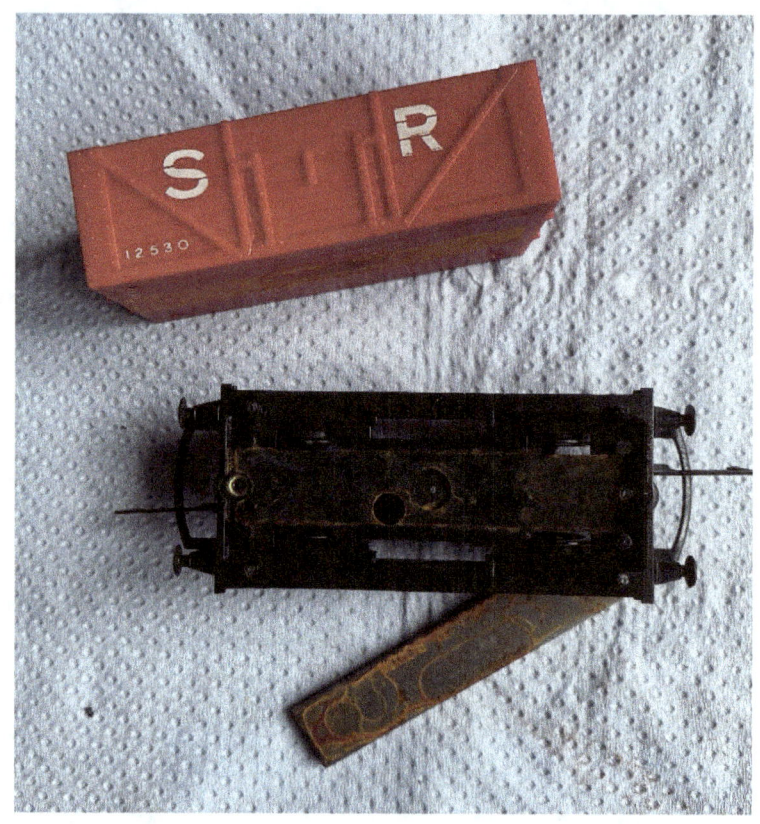

At this stage, it is worth opening out the holes in the body slightly using a small drill bit to aid refitting later. Similarly, burred over post ends can be cut off using sprue cutters.

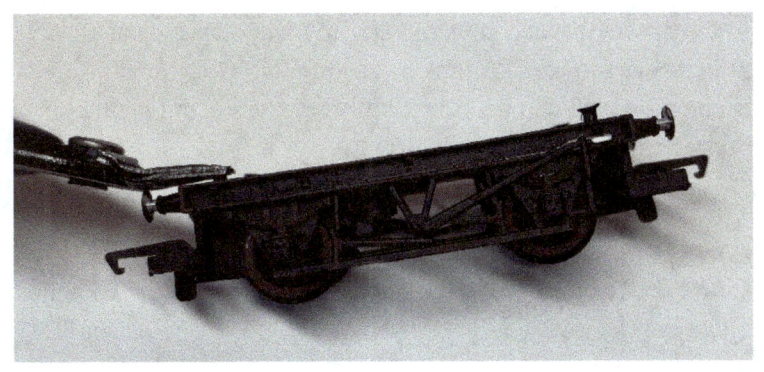

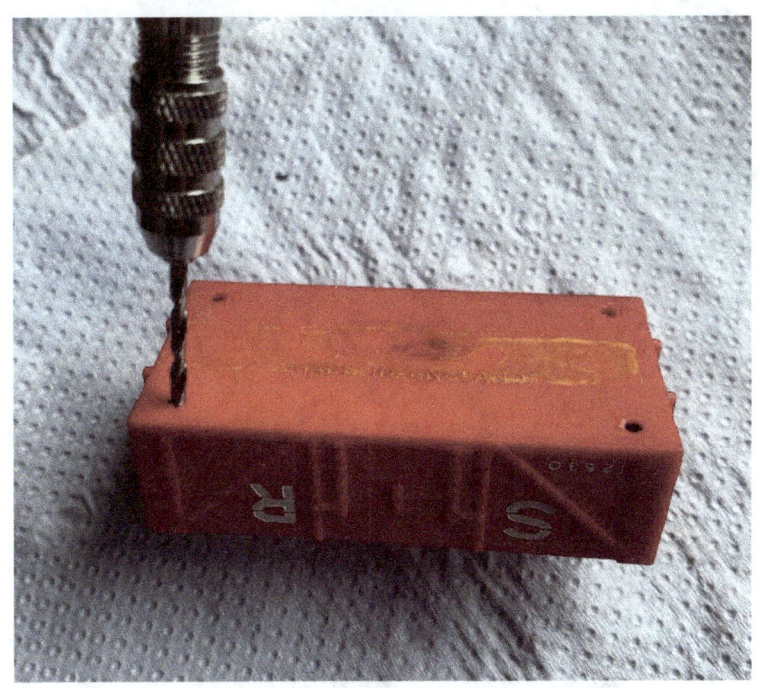

Longer wheelbase Triang and Hornby wagons, such as the 21t mineral wagon or TTA tanker wagon, utilise plastic clips at each end which can be individually released using gentle pressure from a small screwdriver.

Triang Cemflo cement tankers seem to often be glued to the chassis so do not try to remove those too aggressively as, from bitter experience, a broken wagon body or stabbed hand may result!

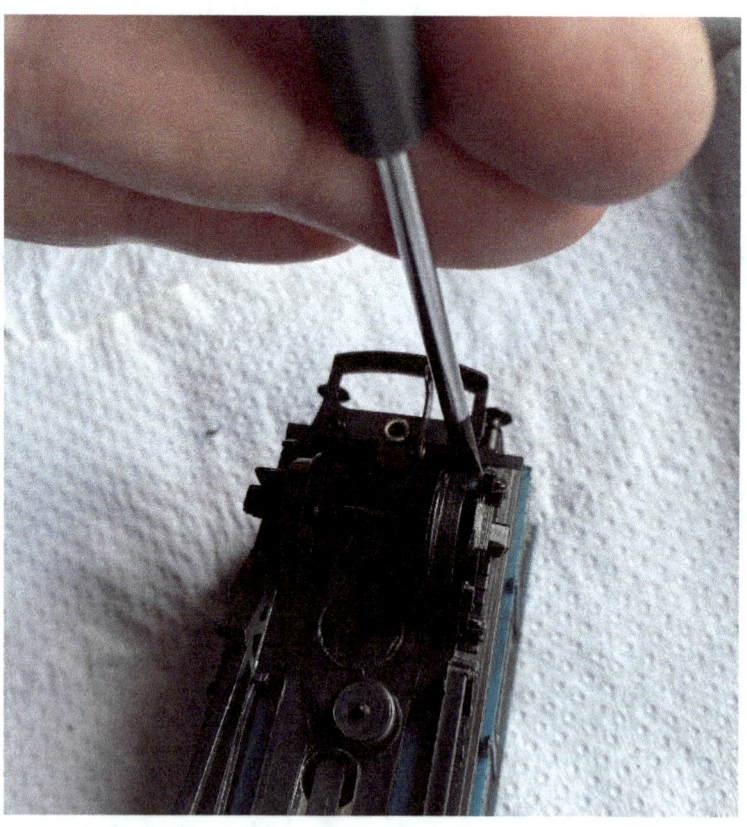

Triang and Hornby brake vans use a similar system, but the clips are on each side of the wagon.

For Triang and Hornby 12t tanker wagons, we do not need to fully separate the body and chassis as the superstructure will be painted along with the chassis. In this case, the tank can simply be released using finger pressure on the end supports in turn.

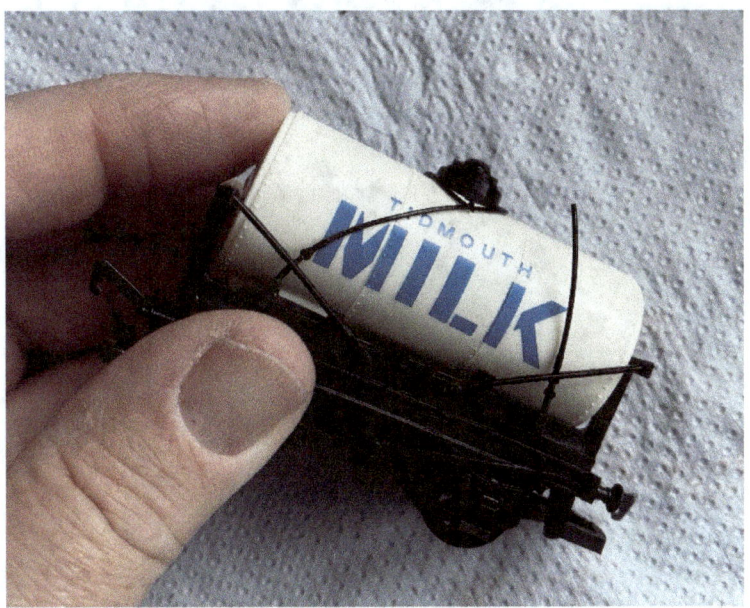

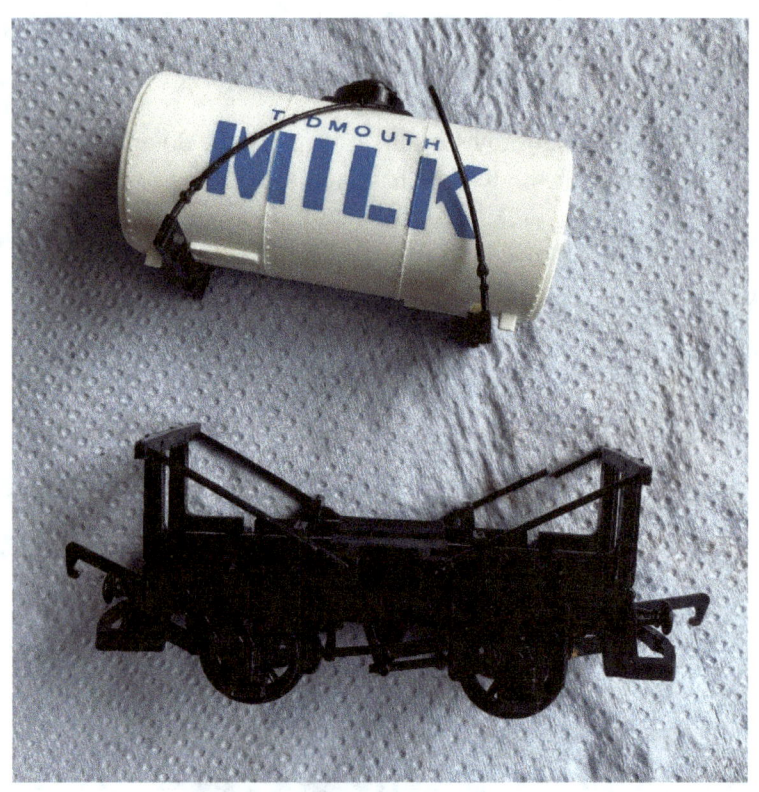

Lima, Mainline and Airfix GMR items tend to be rather more temperamental or even glued in place, so I usually work on those intact. Luckily, the finish on Mainline and Airfix GMR items tends to be far superior to other brands from the era so less extensive work is required in any case.

# Chapter 4 – Lima Plank Wagon (detail painting & weathering)

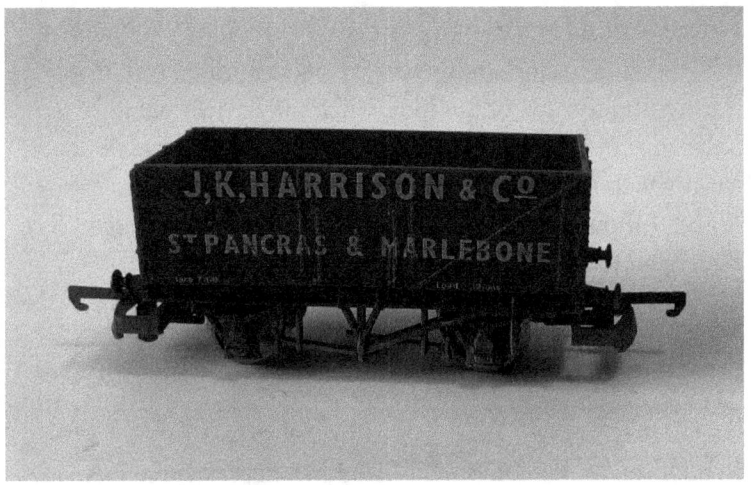

In this first project, we will start off by looking at a fantastically shiny plastic 1970s plank wagon from Lima, a stereotypical "toy train" item, this example set me back the princely sum of £2.25.

Aside from the usual dirt and wear related issues, this particular example also has some silver paint spattered around on the chassis.

The original Lima metal wheels have enormous "pizza cutter" flanges and, if desired, careful use of an axle reamer will allow replacement with Hornby wheel sets which are slightly longer than the Lima items.

But those points aside, it is still possible to make this model into something acceptable for running or just filling up a siding where the latest rolling stock would be too costly to use.

Before starting any painting process, particularly on items of this age, it is important to ensure a clean surface free from greasy fingerprints or the like which may affect paint adhesion. In the case of this wagon, there is nothing delicate to worry about so a good scrub in water and washing up liquid, followed by a thorough rinse, is ideal. The wagon has then been left to air dry for a day.

One suggestion here, you may want to take some photos of the wagon before you start to compare against your finished product.

In addition to the equipment listed in Chapter 2, for this project you will require the following items or suitable equivalents.

| Item | What I used |
|---|---|
| Black acrylic primer | Mig Ammo One Shot Primer |
| Acrylic paint | Mig Ammo, Matt Black |
| Acrylic paint | Mig Ammo, Old Rust |
| Acrylic paint | Mig Ammo, Matt Aluminium |
| Acrylic paint | Vallejo Model Air, White |
| Acrylic paint | Rail Match, Frame Dirt |
| Acrylic varnish, satin | Mig Ammo Lucky Varnish |
| Acrylic varnish, matt | Winsor & Newton Galleria |
| Enamel wash | Mig Ammo, Starship Filth |
| Streaking product | Mig Ammo Oil Brusher, Dark Brown |

| Oil effect | Mig Ammo, Fresh Engine Oil |
|---|---|
| Size 4 brush | |
| Size 5/0 brush | |
| Size 10/0 brush | |
| Size 2/0 brush | |
| Size 10 brush | |

**Step 1**

In order to break up the sea of shiny plastic, the chassis and interior are hand painted with a black acrylic primer using a size 1 to 4 brush. The wheels are also painted with black primer to aid later painting.

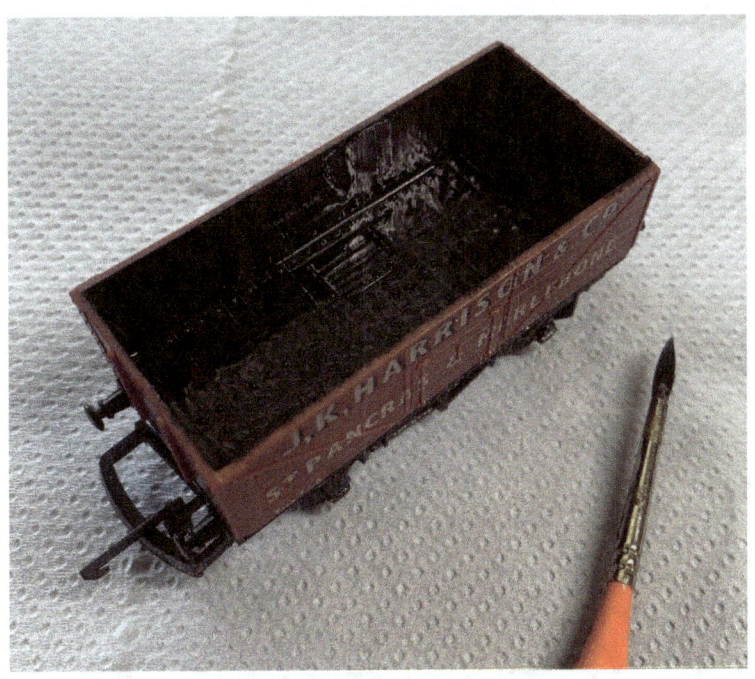

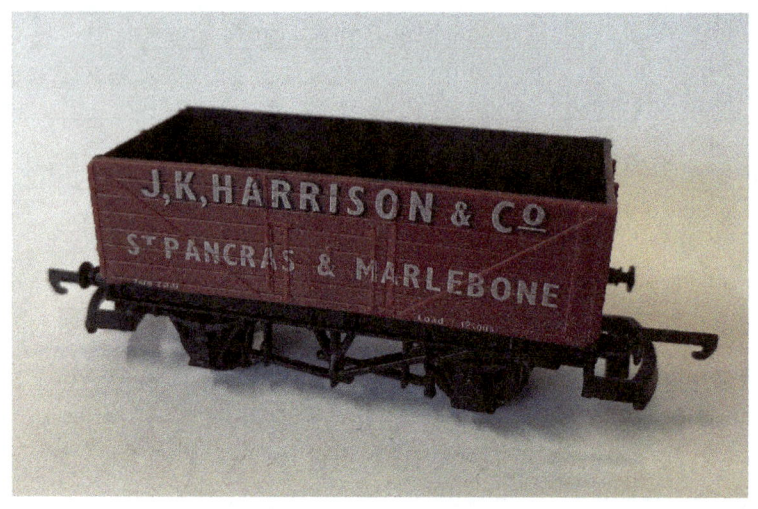

**Step 2**

Once dry, this is followed by picking out steelwork in matt black acrylic paint using a size 5/0 brush.

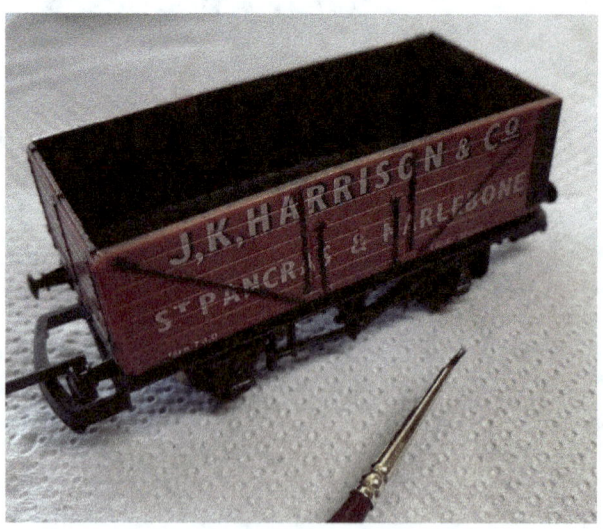

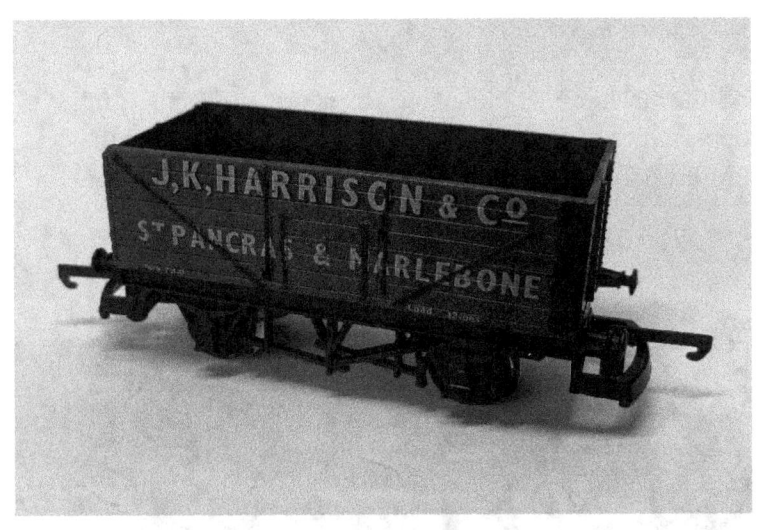

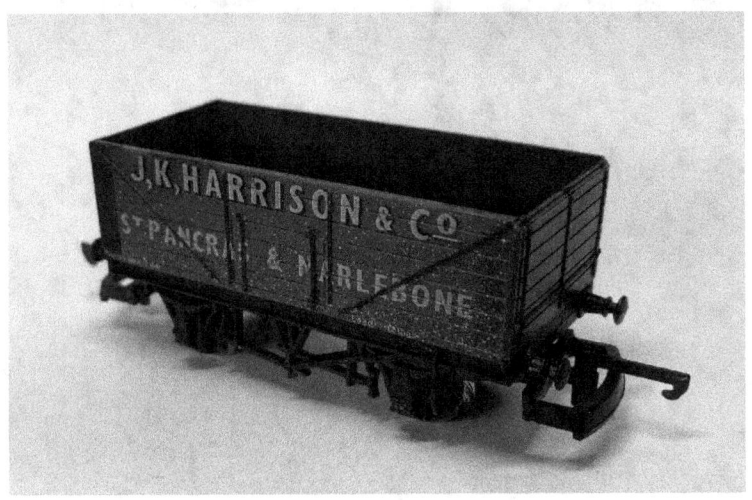

**Step 3**

As the black primer on the chassis is dry, we can take this opportunity to apply our silver colour acrylic paint to the buffer shafts.

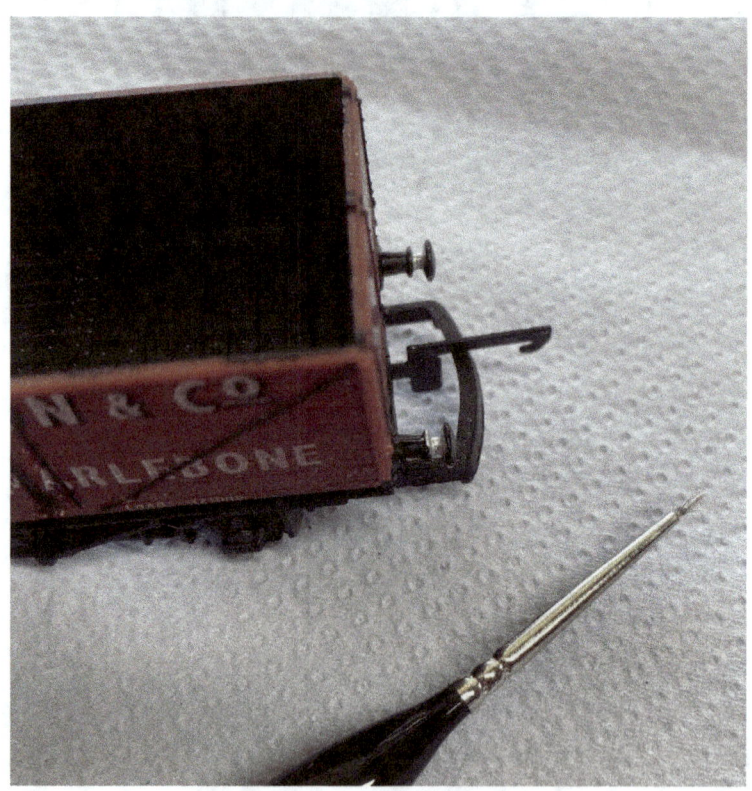

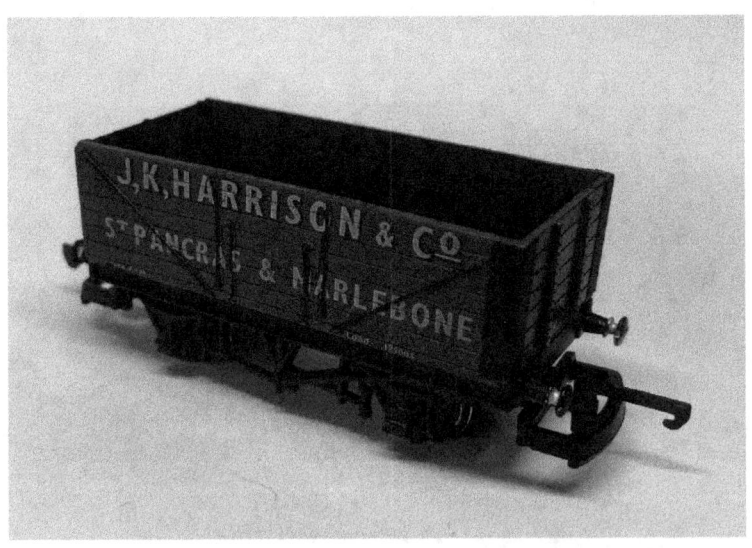

**Step 4**

Once the black acrylic on the ironwork is dry, we can continue by hand painting rusty paint chips onto the chassis and ironwork using a 5/0 or 10/0 brush.

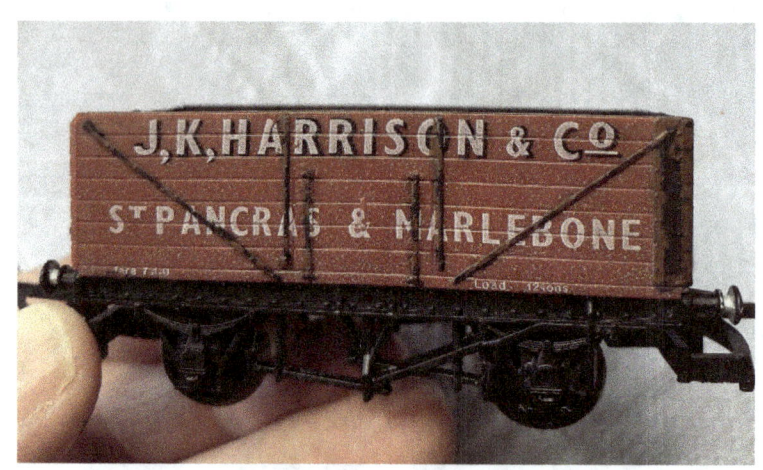

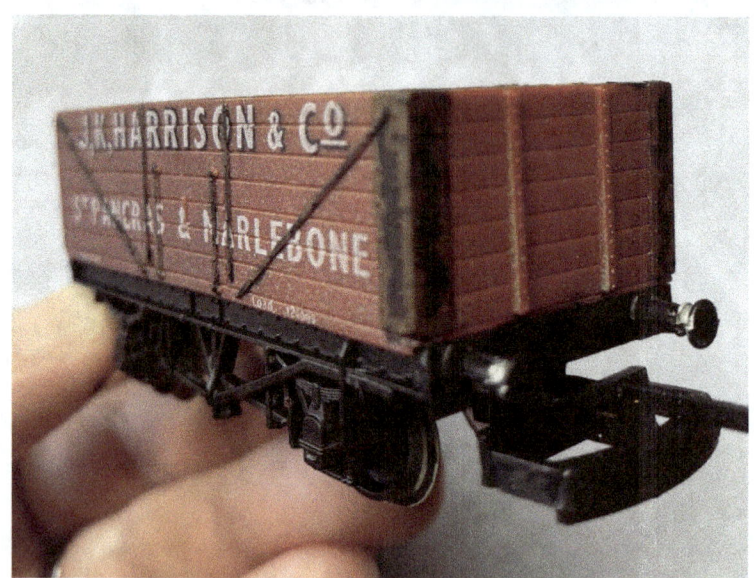

**Step 5**

The wheels can then be painted in rust colour using a 2/0 brush. Picking out cast iron brake shoes and leaf springs with the rust colour helps break up the chassis colour.

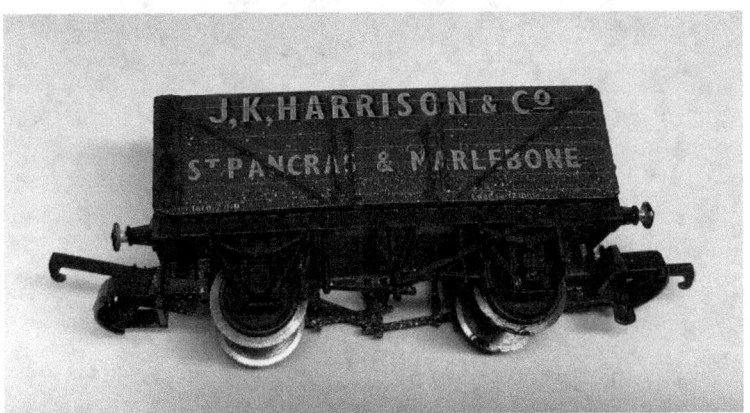

**Step 6**

This is followed by picking out the brake handles in white acrylic.

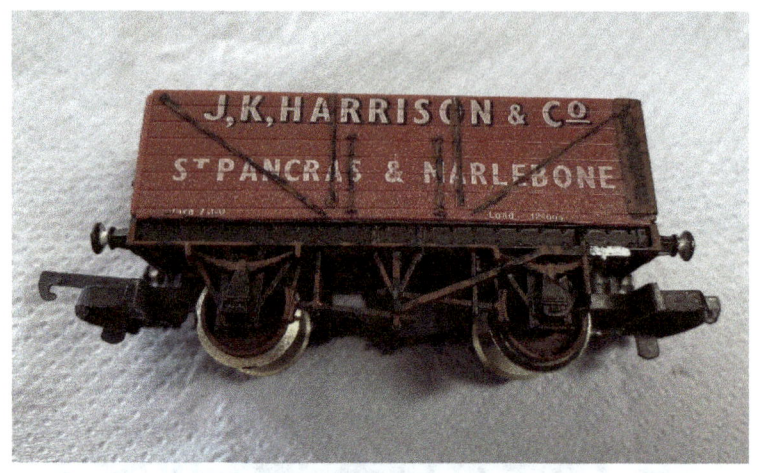

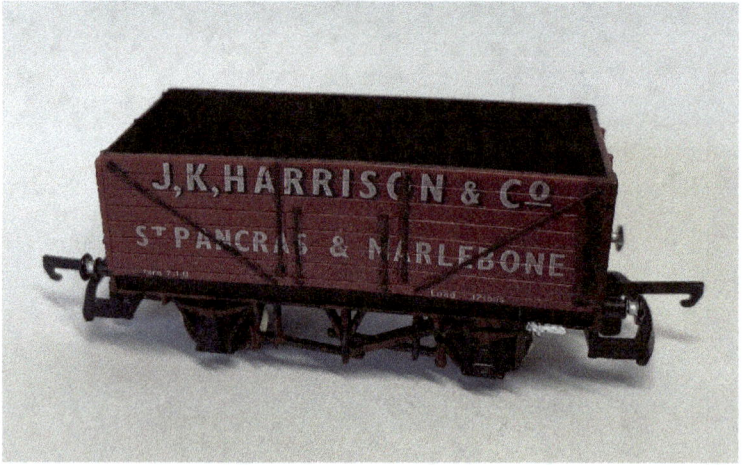

As you can see, even at this stage the wagon is starting to look less toy-like and will give a good basis for the weathering stages to come.

**Step 7**

Once the acrylic paint applied in Step 1 is fully dry, we need to protect our work from the aggressive solvent-based weathering products that we will be using from Step 3 onwards. In order to achieve this, we need to apply a coat of acrylic varnish as a barrier layer using the airbrush. For this stage, a satin varnish is used to allow the enamel washes to readily flow along moulded lines on the model.

Once coated, allow the varnish to fully cure for 24 hours to provide full protection of the paintwork below.

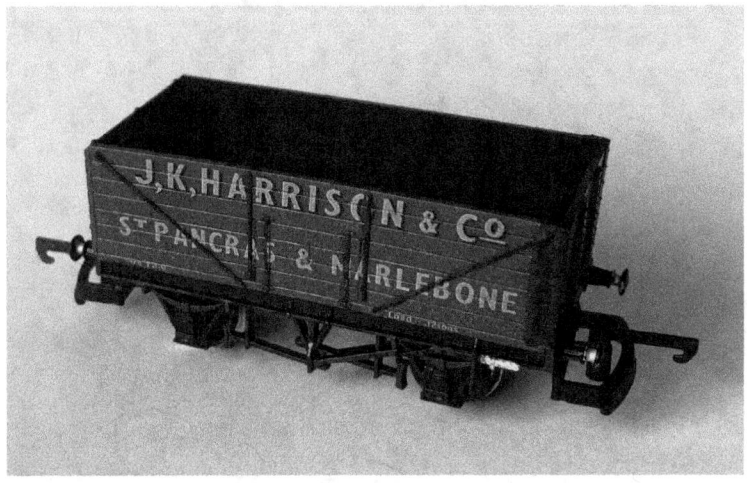

**Step 8**

In order to bring out the moulded detail of the model and provide a base level of dirt on the body, we now need to apply a suitably coloured enamel wash.

The colour selection needs to be driven by the base colour of the wagon as only light-coloured deposits will be visible on dark coloured wagons and vice versa. In this case, I have used a dark grey wash suited to strongly coloured models.

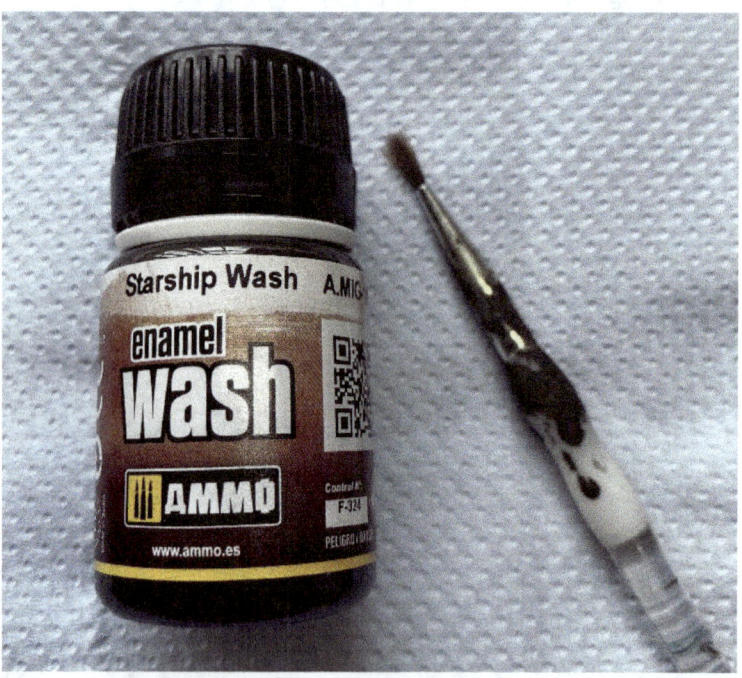

Using a 2/0 brush, apply the well shaken enamel wash to each raised or recessed detail on the wagon body and allow the wash to flow along the moulded edges. Tilting the wagon as you apply the wash will allow gravity to assist the flow of the wash. Do not completely smother the whole model in wash, this just wastes wash as the majority will be removed in the next step.

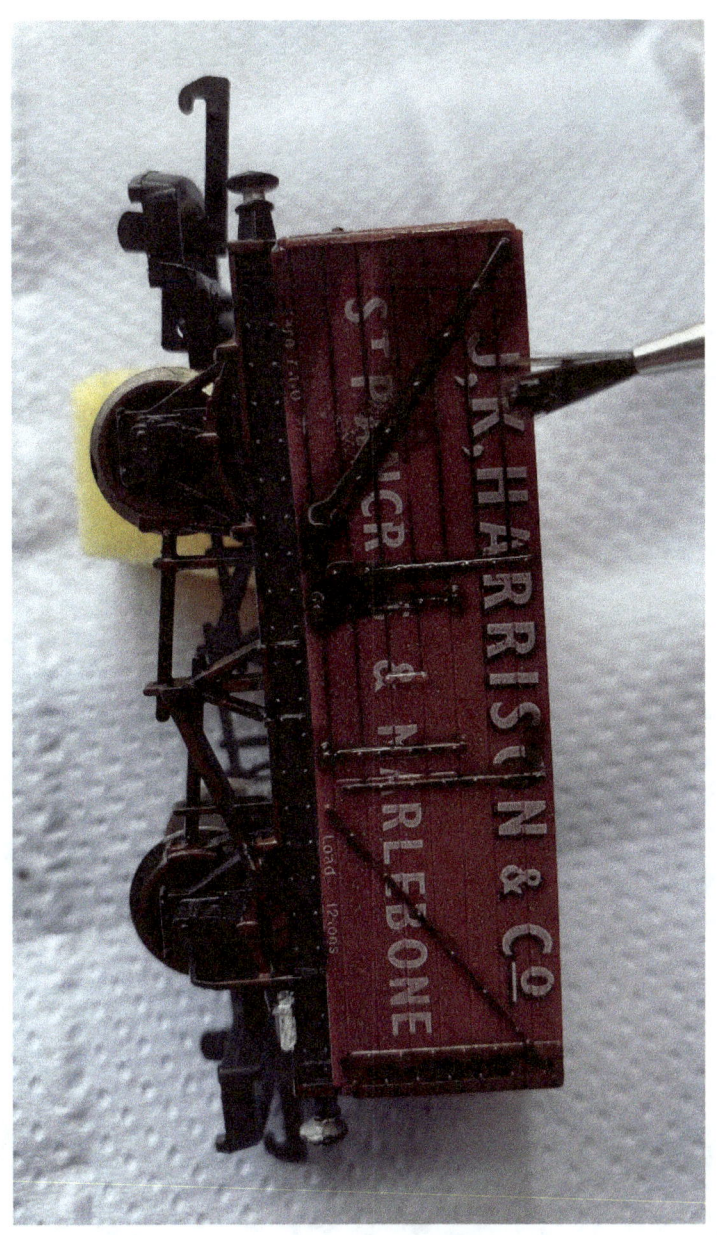

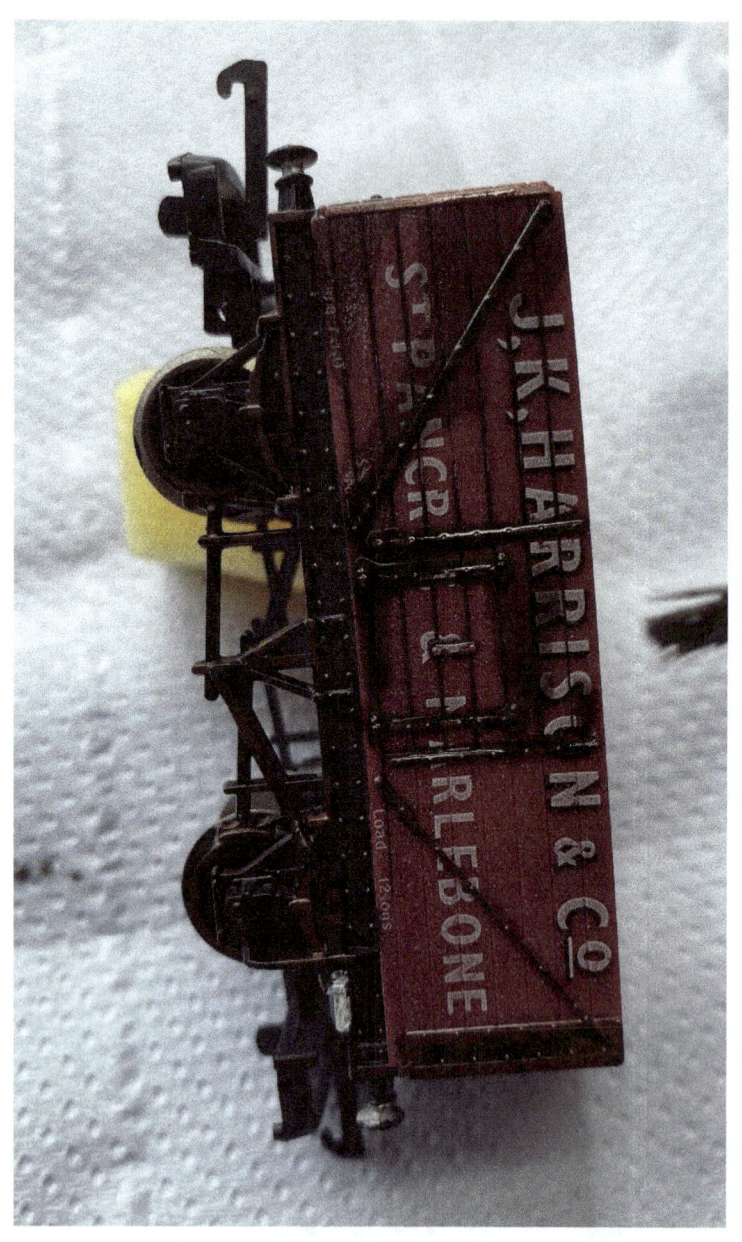

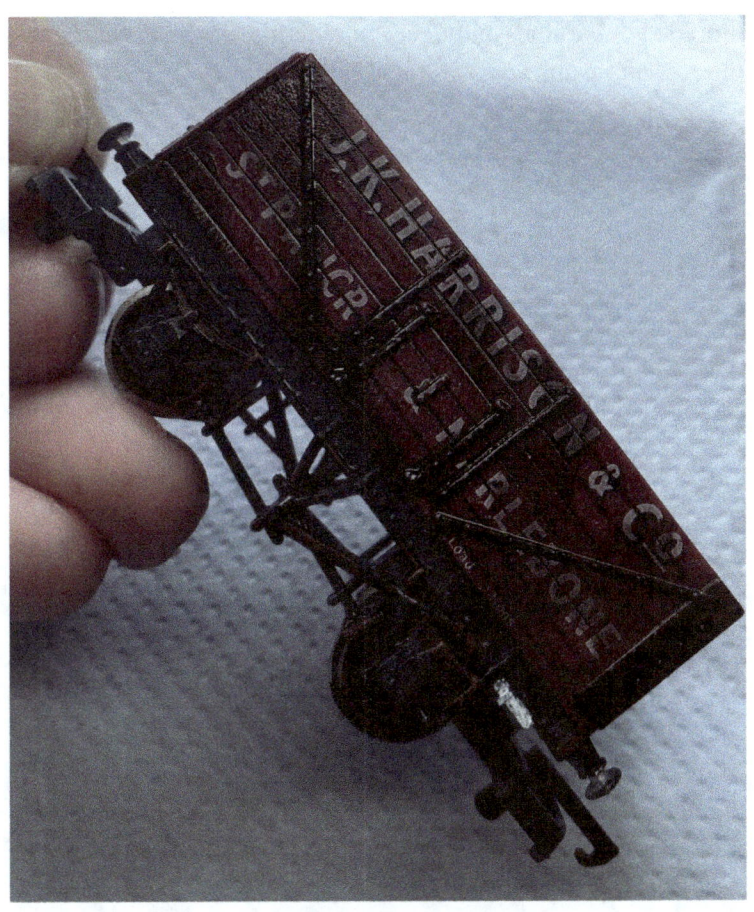

Leave the wash to dry for around 30 minutes.

**Step 9**

Once the wash has dried sufficiently, it is time to remove the excess wash. This needs to be done carefully to avoid removing too much wash, we want to leave the colour in the moulded detail lines and have some feint dirt streaks across the rest of the surface.

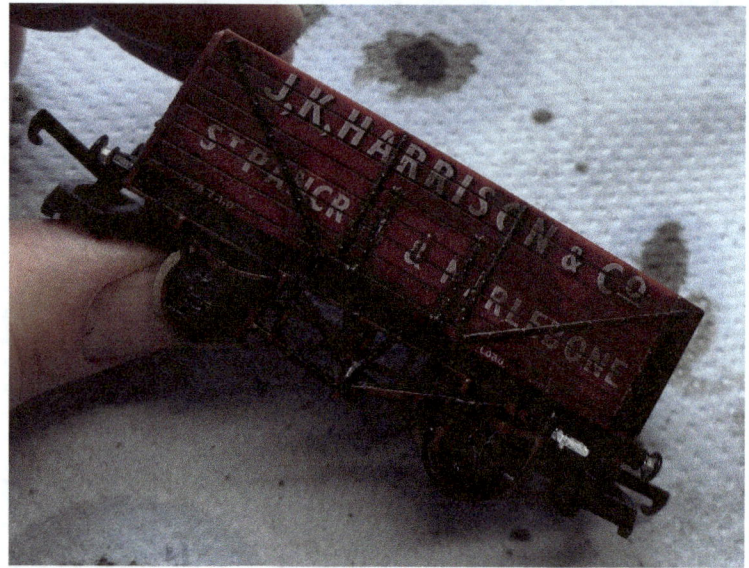

To remove the wash, use a broad tipped size 10 brush (moistened in odourless enamel thinners, if necessary, and then dried on some paper towel (there should be no thinners transferred to the model surface from the brush)).

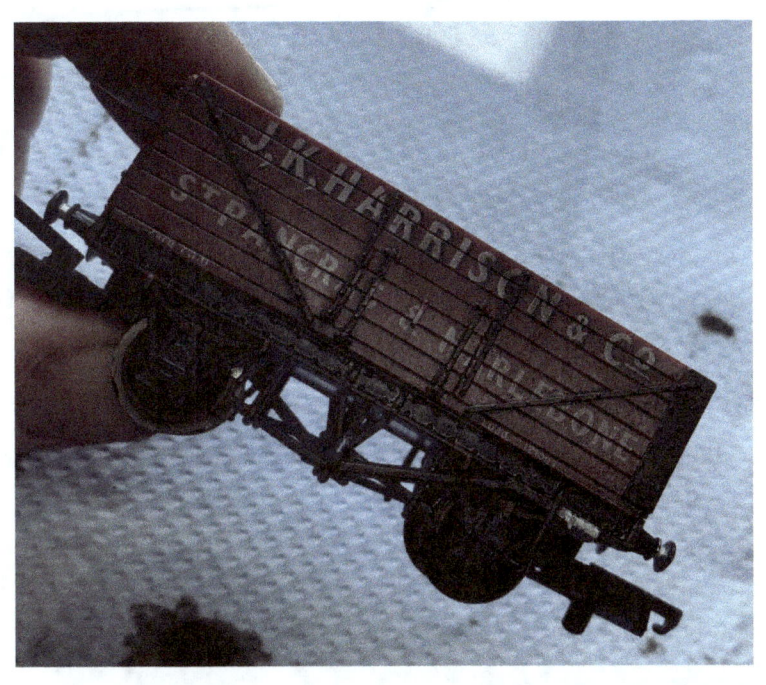

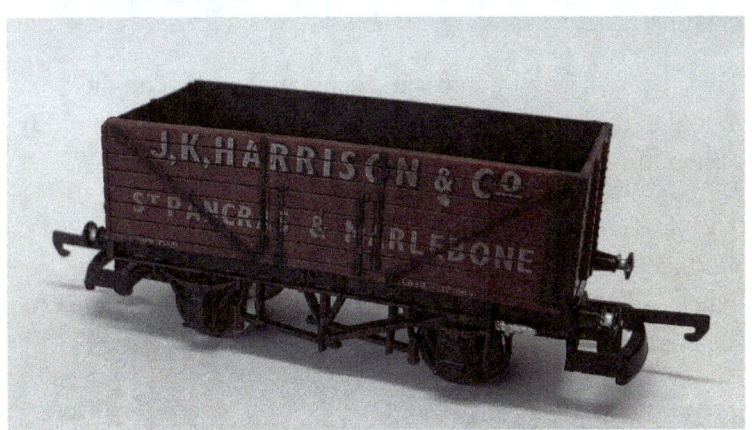

47

Then, ensuring that you only work vertically down the sides of the model to mimic rain effects, gently draw the brush across the washed areas and wipe excess from the brush onto the paper towel. There should be no need to remoisten the brush for a model of this size.

Do not worry if you are not happy with the result! The enamel wash can be remobilised with a brush moistened in thinners and, if too much wash is removed, you can apply more and try again. The use of enamel-based wash makes this quite a forgiving process, just try to avoid rubbing through the varnish layer underneath.

Once fully dry, after 24 hours, the wagon should now have more pronounced detail and is starting to look more realistically dirty. Avoid handling the dried wash areas as finger marks are very easily made on the unprotected surface.

**Step 10**

This step will provide further accentuation of dirt on the model in the form of streaks, these will break up the currently rather uniform dirt effect on the wagon body.

The streaking effects are achieved using an oil paint-based product (not standard oil paints, which require removal of excess oil prior to use) and works in a very similar fashion to the enamel wash used earlier.

The choice of streaking colour needs to be determined from the likely use that the wagon received, in this case as it is a coal wagon, I have used a very dark brown product as black is a little too intense. Rust is also a useful streaking colour on heavily weathered models, but I have not applied rust streaks in this example.

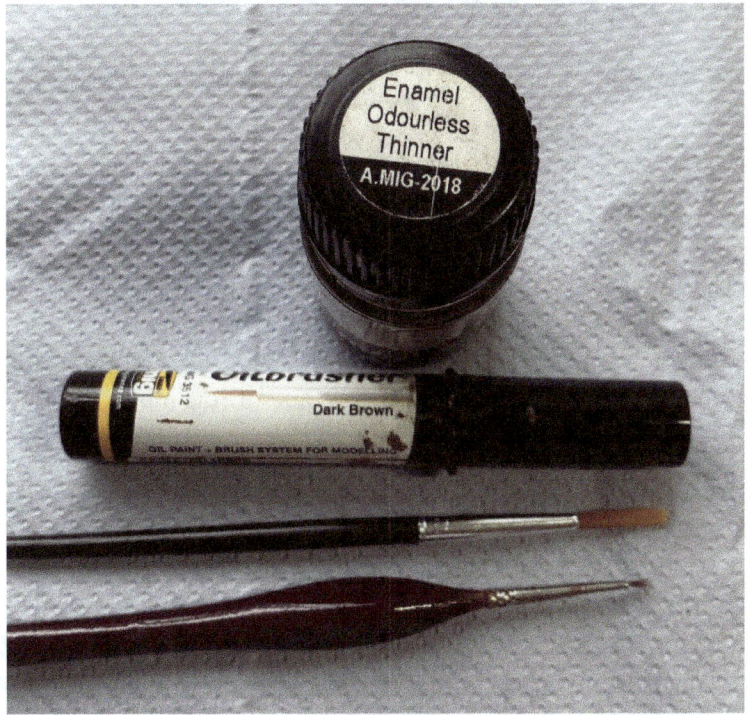

To create the dirt streaks, using a 5/0 brush place a very fine stripe of the streaking product running down from the start point you want.

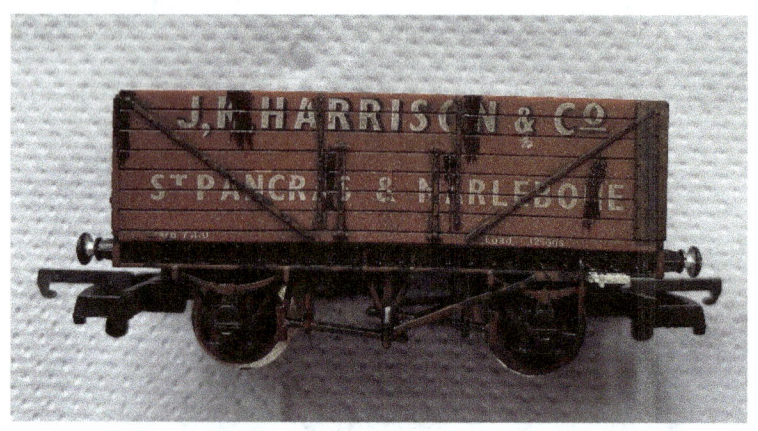

Then, using a size 2/0 to 4 round brush moistened in enamel thinner, begin to drag product down and off the model. Frequently wiping the brush on some paper towel to removed excess oil paint.

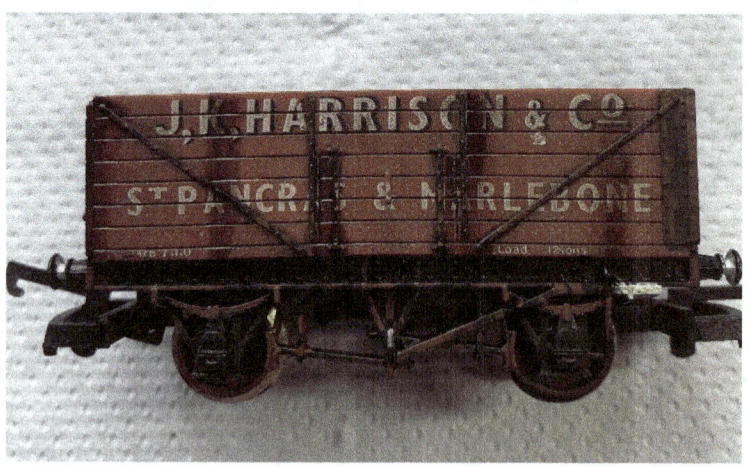

Continue streaking the product down using the moistened brush until you are happy with the effect and then leave to dry for 24 hours.

**Step 11**

Now that the wagon is looking rather more detailed, we can use the airbrush to apply a misted coat of our chosen dirt colour to the chassis and lower regions of the wagon body to imitate the splashed dirt from the track and ballast. The wagon body ends are also worth attention as these tend to accumulate more dirt than the sides.

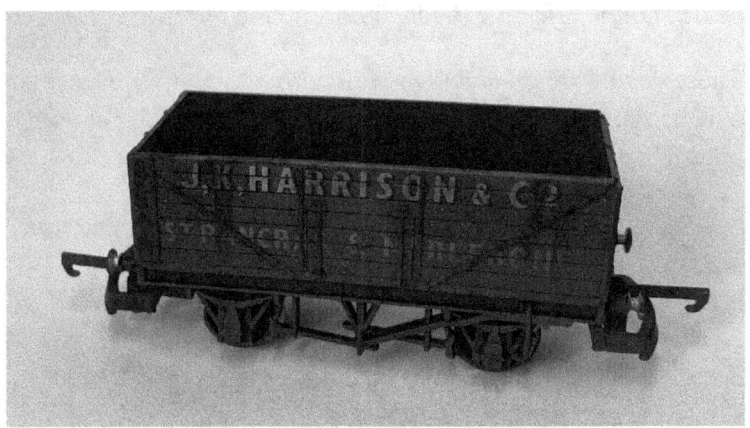

**Step 12**

This step is entirely optional, but for my example I decided that a load in the wagon would add to the weathering effects.

I sourced a suitably sized resin cast coal load and spray painted it matt black using a generic car spray paint, it can obviously be painted using the airbrush if desired.

The desired height for the load was achieved by using a cut piece of packing foam placed below the resin cast load.

## Step 13

To provide protection of our weathered surfaces and remove any remaining sheen from the plastic, the model now needs to be given two coats of matt acrylic varnish using the airbrush.

## Step 14

The final stage involves adding minor details over the matt varnish which need to retain a satin or gloss sheen and would, hence, not be effective if added prior to the matt varnish.

These details are oil and grease effects on the buffer ends and axle bearing boxes, applied using a 5/0 brush and our chosen oil effect product.

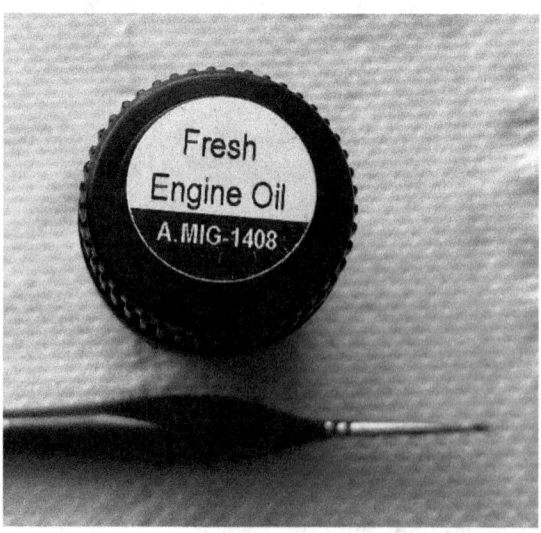

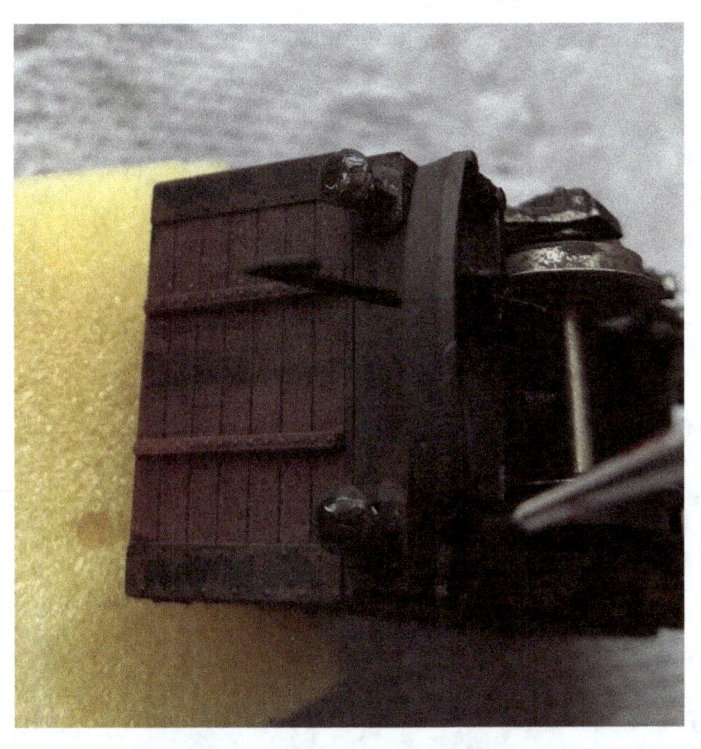

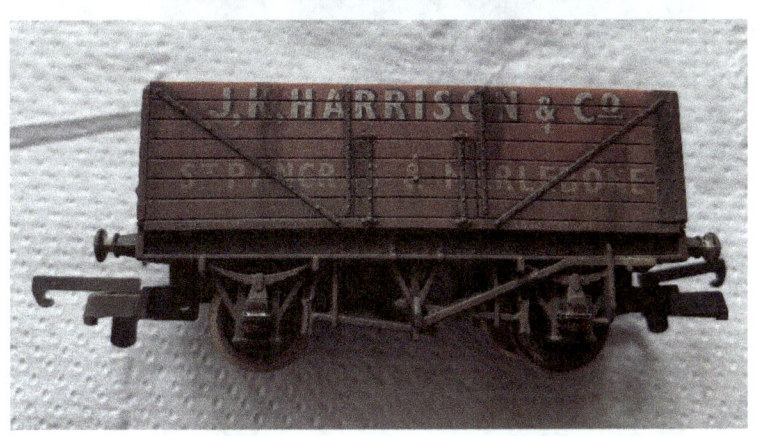

53

Once dry, the model is complete and should look strikingly different to how it started!

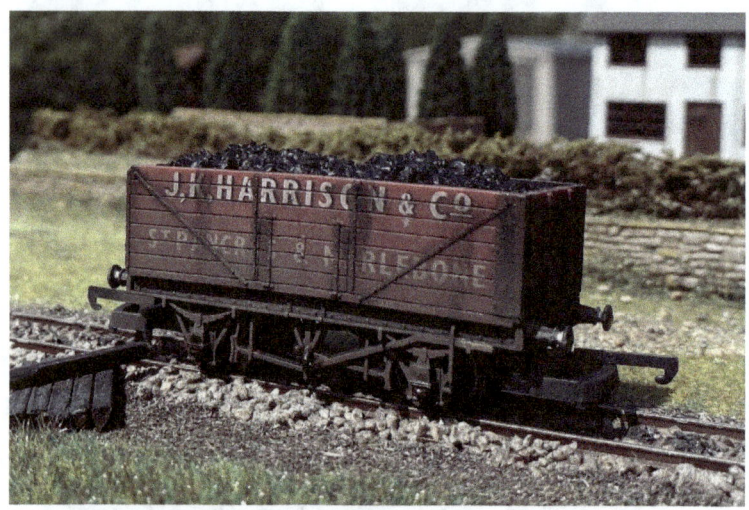

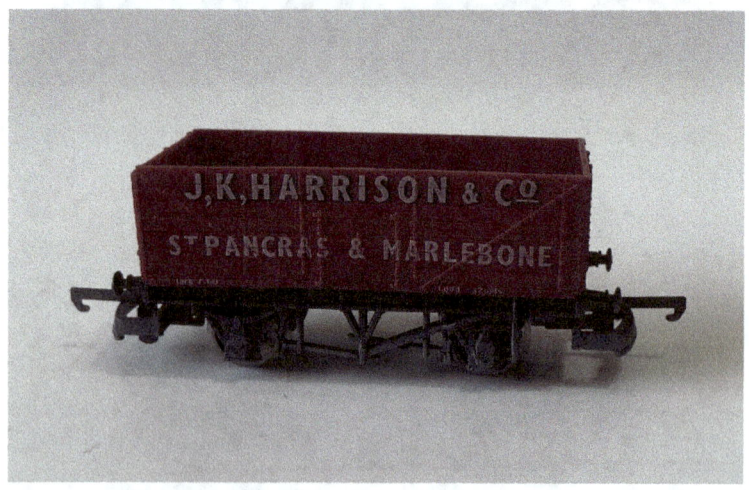

# Chapter 5 – Mainline Plank Wagon (oil paint fading & weathering)

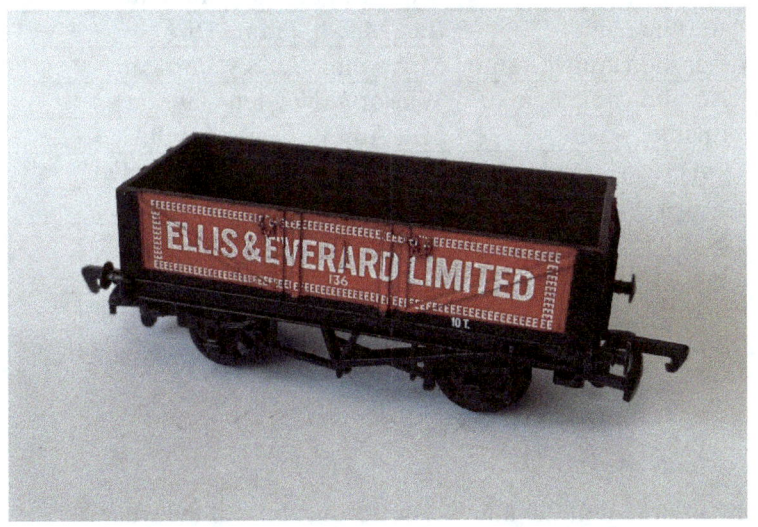

In this project, we will be working on a Mainline plank wagon, dating to the 1970s and 1980s.

Rather than a scrub in soapy water, this model was cleaned with a dry brush as it just appeared to be a little dusty.

In addition to the equipment listed in Chapter 2, for this project you will require the following items or suitable equivalents.

| Item | What I used |
|---|---|
| Oil Brusher | Mig Ammo, Dust |
| Acrylic paint | Mig Ammo, Old Rust |
| Acrylic paint | Mig Ammo, White |
| Acrylic paint | Mig Ammo, Matt Aluminium |
| Acrylic paint | Rail Match, Frame Dirt |
| Acrylic varnish, satin | Mig Ammo Lucky Varnish |
| Acrylic varnish, matt | Winsor & Newton Galleria |
| Enamel wash | Mig Ammo, Starship Filth |
| Oil effect | Mig Ammo, Fresh Engine Oil |
| Size 4 brush | |
| Size 5/0 brush | |
| Size 10/0 brush | |
| Size 2/0 brush | |
| Size 10 brush | |

**Step 1**

In order to dull the intense, uniform colour of the wagon planking we will start off by applying an oil paint filter to the outside surface to mimic sun fading of the paintwork.

Using an Oil Brusher type product this is a simple but very effective process which will make an immediate improvement to the wagon's appearance.

Using the built-in brush, place small spots on each face of the wagon, usually around 4 or 5 will be sufficient on each face but it will become apparent if too little or too much has been applied and that can be addressed as work progresses.

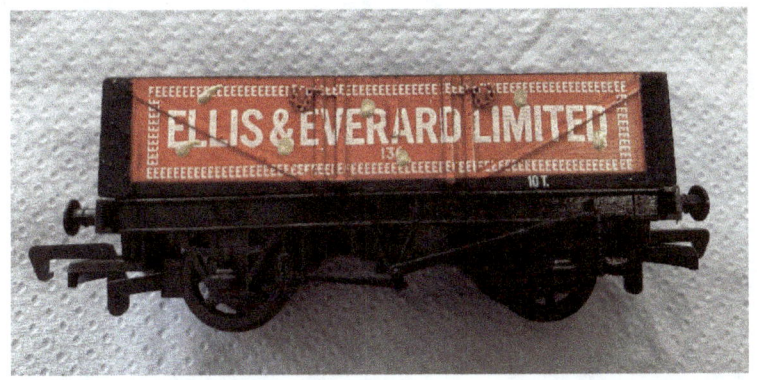

Using a Size 10 brush, work the oil paint over the outer surface of the wagon using a circular motion until the entire surface is covered with a fine film of oil paint (add more dots of paint if insufficient is present). Once completely covered, wipe the brush on some paper towel and proceed to remove further oil paint from the wagon surface using vertical downward strokes and repeated wiping of the brush on the paper towel. Using a folded paper towel, carefully remove oil paint from the wagon ironwork parts and chassis (this will aid later painting steps).

Once complete, the surface should look discoloured but not obscured by excessive paint.

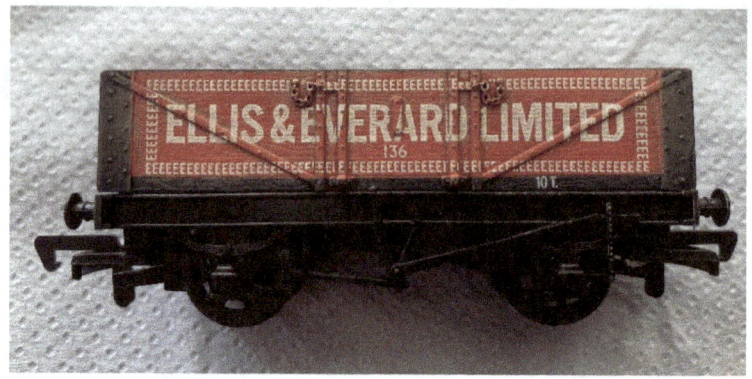

Leave the oil paint for 48 hours to dry thoroughly.

**Step 2**

This is followed by hand painting rusty paint chips onto the chassis and ironwork using a 5/0 or 10/0 brush.

The wheels were painted in rust colour using a 2/0 brush. Picking out cast iron brake shoes and leaf springs with the rust colour helps break up the chassis colour.

**Step 3**

The final painting stage involves picking out the buffer shafts in our silver acrylic colour and the brake lever handles using white acrylic using a 5/0 or 10/0 brush.

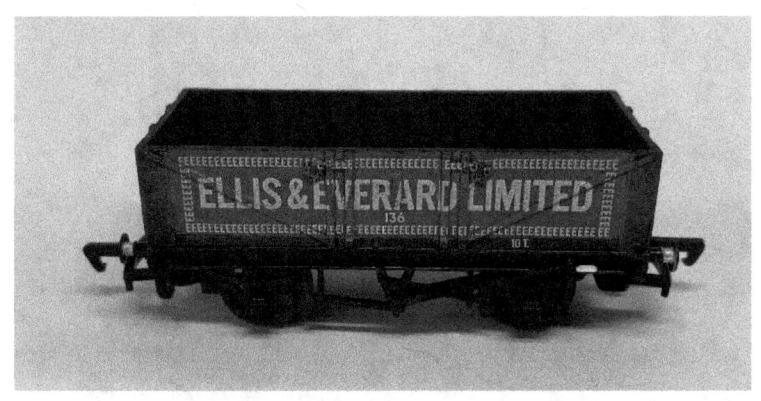

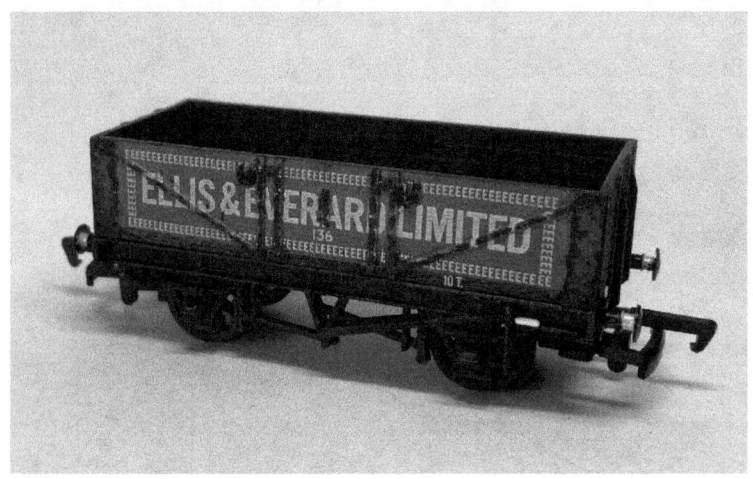

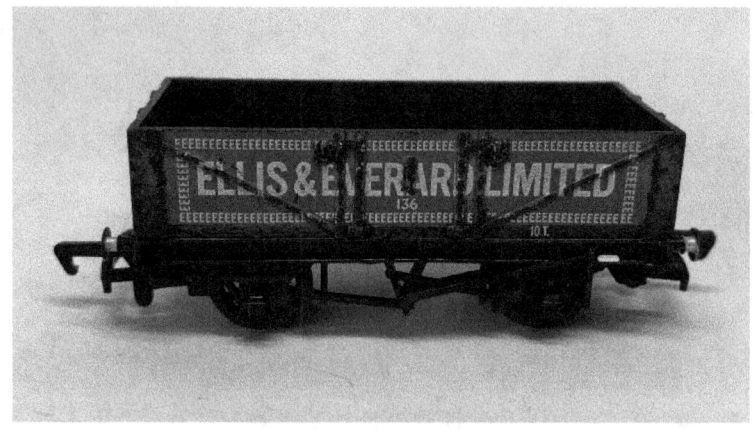

**Step 4**

Once the acrylic paint is fully dry, we will apply a coat of satin acrylic varnish as a barrier layer using the airbrush.

Allow the varnish to fully cure for 24 hours to provide full protection of the paintwork below.

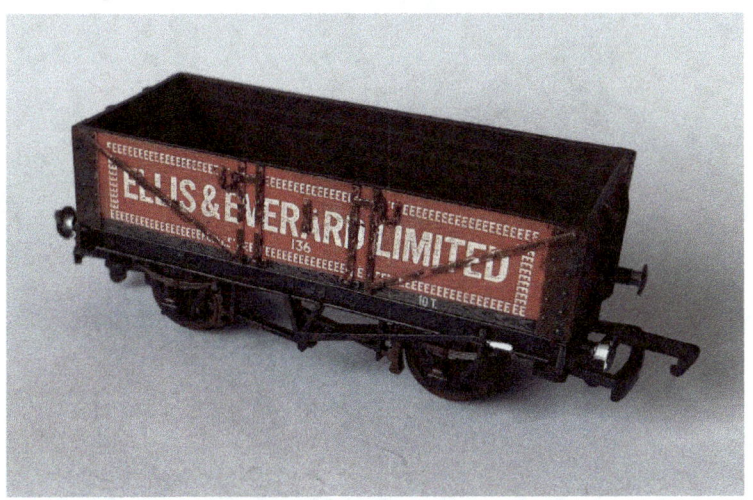

**Step 5**

We now need to apply a suitably coloured enamel wash, as we are dealing with a coal again, I have stuck with the same wash used earlier.

Using a 2/0 brush, apply the well shaken enamel wash to each raised or recessed detail on the wagon body and allow the wash to flow along the moulded edges. Tilting the wagon as you apply the wash will allow gravity to assist the flow of the wash. Do not completely smother the whole model in wash, this just wastes wash as the majority will be removed in the next step.

Leave the wash to dry for around 30 minutes.

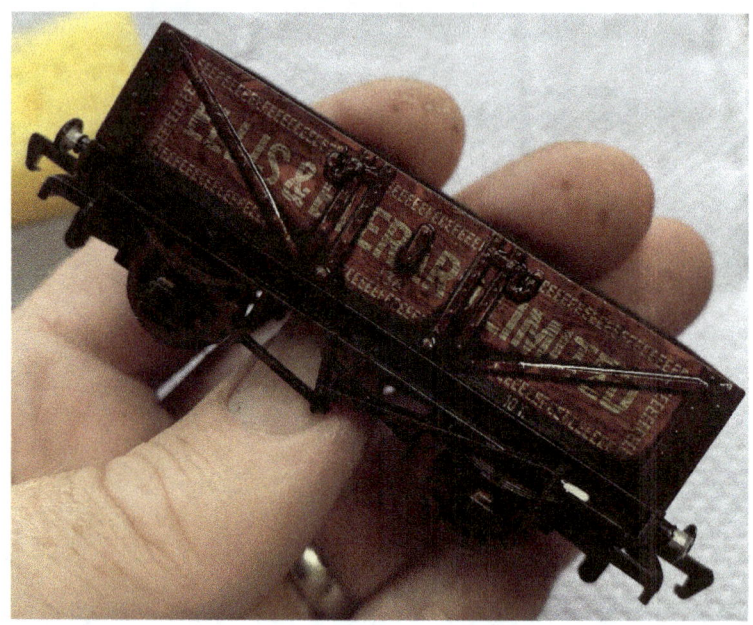

**Step 6**

Once the wash has dried sufficiently, as done in Chapter 3, remove the excess wash using a broad tipped size 10 brush.

Leave to dry for 24 hours.

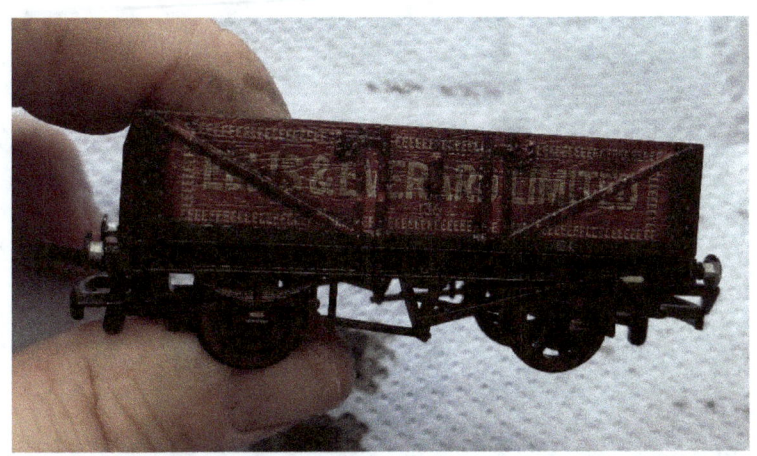

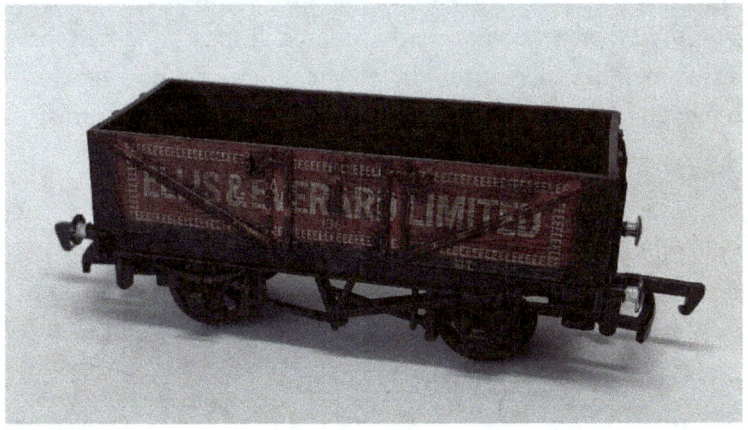

**Step 7**

I have omitted additional streaking from this model, and we will move on to adding frame dirt.

Use the airbrush to apply a misted coat of our chosen dirt colour to the chassis and lower regions of the wagon body and body ends.

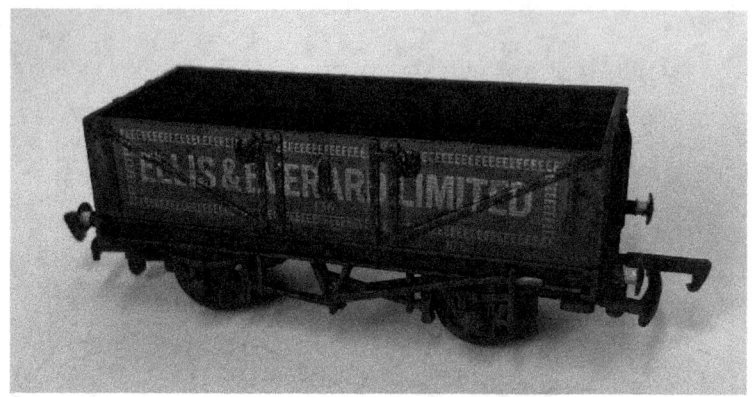

**Step 8**

To provide protection of our weathered surfaces and remove any remaining sheen from the plastic, the model now needs to be given two coats of matt acrylic varnish using the airbrush.

**Step 9**

Add oil and grease effects on the buffer ends and axle bearing boxes, applied using a 5/0 brush and our chosen oil effect product.

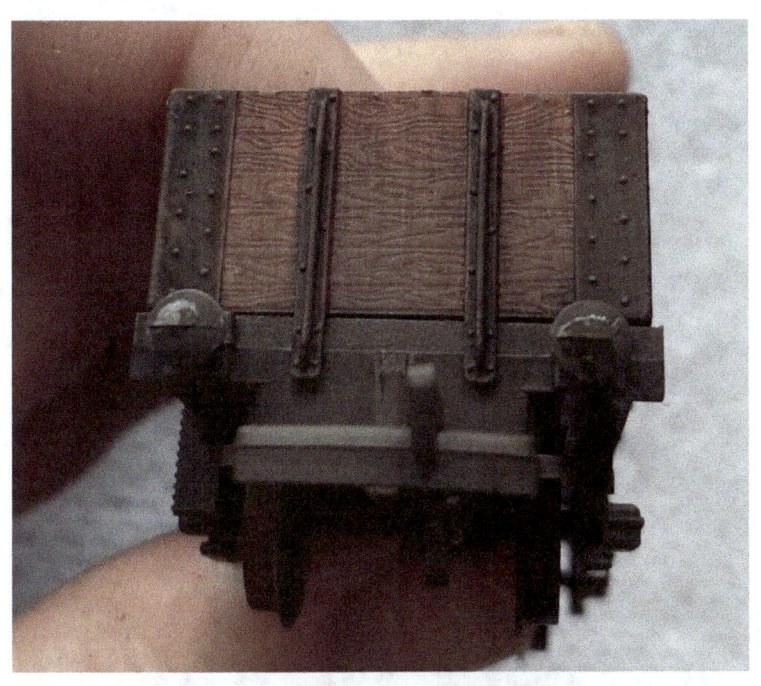

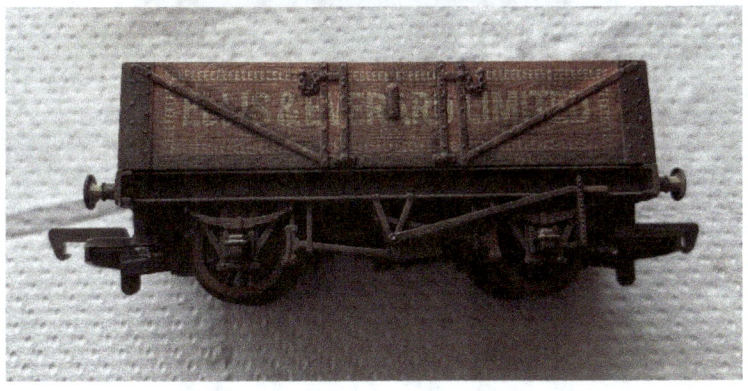

Once dry the improvement against the original paint finish should be obvious.

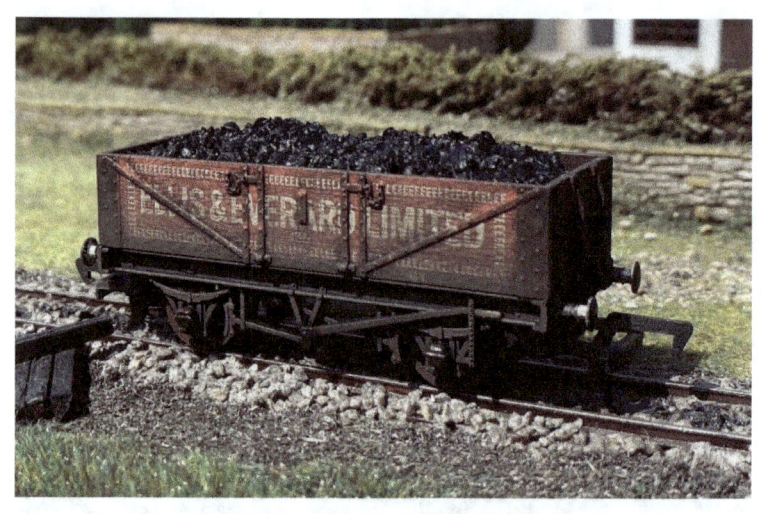

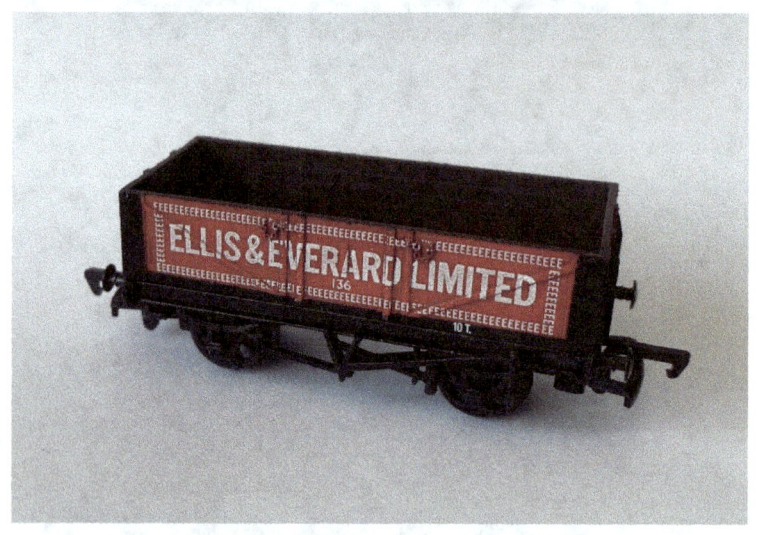

# Chapter 6 – Hornby 20t Brake Van (partial painting & weathering, dot filter on roof)

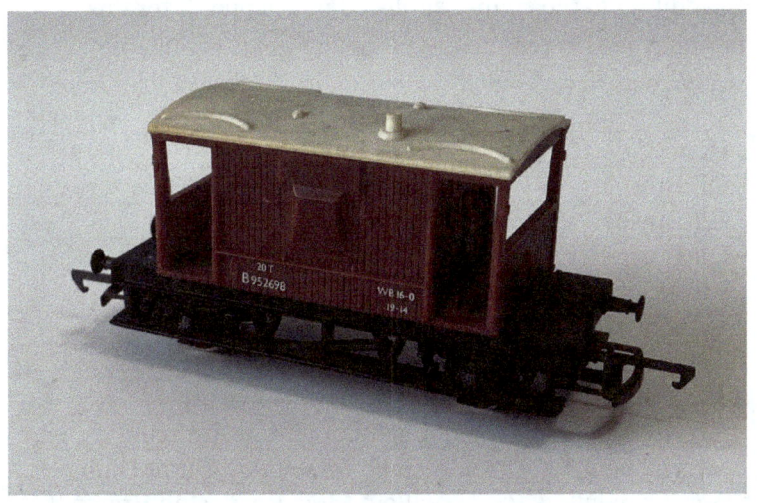

For this project, we will be working on the ubiquitous Hornby 20t brake van, which has been in production from the 1970s to the present day and seems to be available in vast numbers as a used item.

These are, generally, a suitable candidate for a full respray but that option is covered by a later chapter.

As usual, before starting the painting process, the wagon will get a scrub in water and washing up liquid, followed by a thorough rinse and left to air dry for a day. Again, the body can be carefully prised from the chassis to be dealt with separately.

A word of warning - do not try to remove the roof, Hornby and Triang brake van roofs are, generally, glued in place.

In addition to the equipment listed in Chapter 2, for this project you will require the following items or suitable equivalents.

| Item | What I used |
|---|---|
| Oil Brusher | Mig Ammo, Medium Grey |
| Oil Brusher | Mig Ammo, Dark Brown |
| Oil Brusher | Mig Ammo, Star ship Filth |
| Brown acrylic primer | AK surface primer, Rust |
| Acrylic paint | Mig Ammo, Rubber & Tyres |
| Acrylic paint | Mig Ammo, Old Rust |
| Acrylic paint | Mig Ammo, White |
| Acrylic paint | Mig Ammo, Matt Aluminium |
| Acrylic paint | Vallejo Model Air, Burnt Umber |
| Acrylic paint | Vallejo Model Air, Mud Brown |
| Acrylic paint | Rail Match, Frame Dirt |
| Acrylic varnish, satin | Mig Ammo Lucky Varnish |
| Acrylic varnish, matt | Winsor & Newton Galleria |
| Enamel wash | Mig Ammo, Star ship Wash |
| Oil effect | Mig Ammo, Fresh Engine Oil |
| Size 4 brush | |
| Size 5/0 brush | |
| Size 10/0 brush | |
| Size 2/0 brush | |
| Size 10 brush | |

**Step 1**

In order to dull the colour and sheen of the plastic body, we will first apply an acrylic wash to the body walls using a colour that approximates well to BR Bauxite brown. This wash coat is produced by mixing a few drops of Vallejo mud brown with tap water in the pallet, a ratio around 4 drops paint to 2 drops water should work (trial and error will show what works best for you; too much paint in the mix will cake the surface of the body, too much water will result in wash shrinking into droplets on the surface).

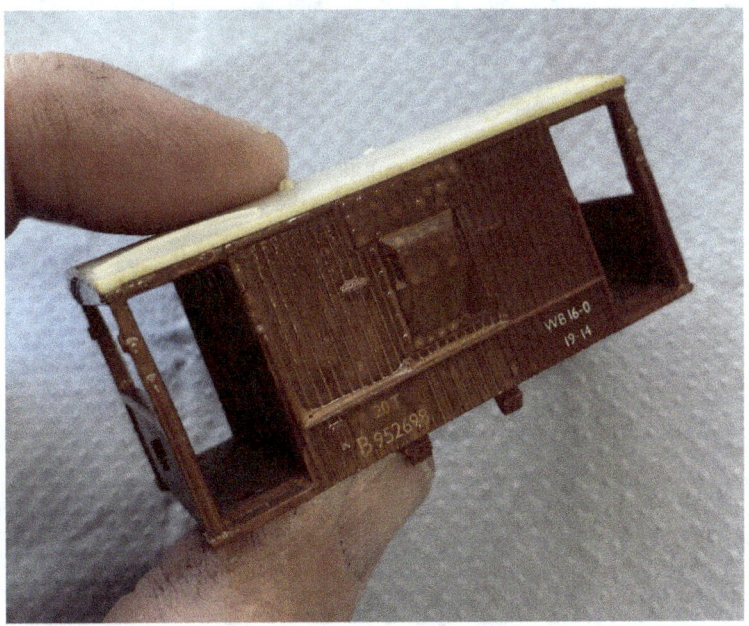

Using a Size 4 brush, evenly coat all the body walls with this wash. Use a dry brush to wick away collected pools of wash before allowing to dry fully.

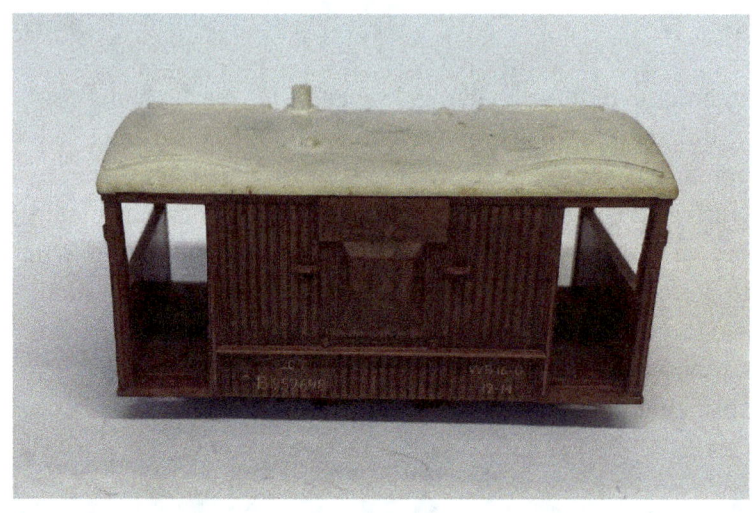

**Step 2**

While the wash is drying, the chassis can be sprayed with a black primer or matt black acrylic spray paint.

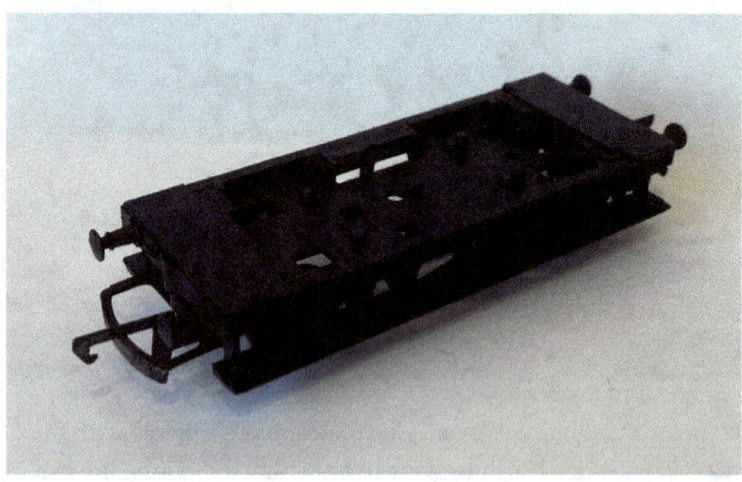

## Step 3

While the wash is drying, the roof can be hand painted with a rust acrylic primer using a size 4 brush.

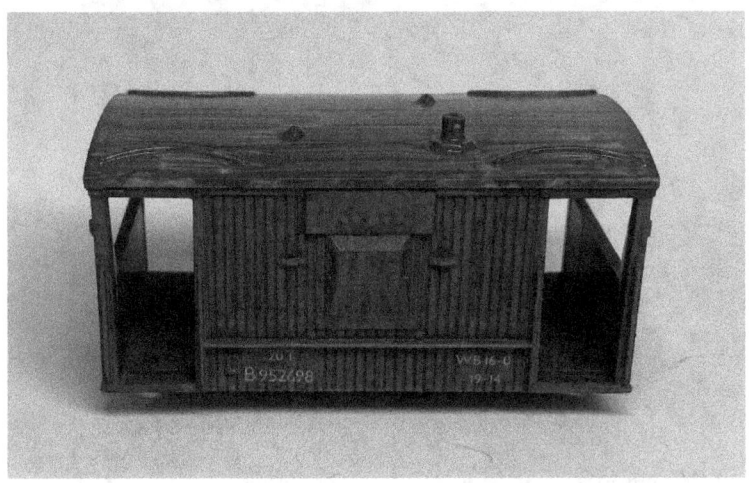

## Step 4

Once the primer is dry, the roof can be hand painted with our grey acrylic paint using a size 4 brush. The roof can be carefully airbrushed rather than hand painted if you feel confident enough, but care needs to be taken to orientate the wagon to avoid overspray onto the walls or chassis.

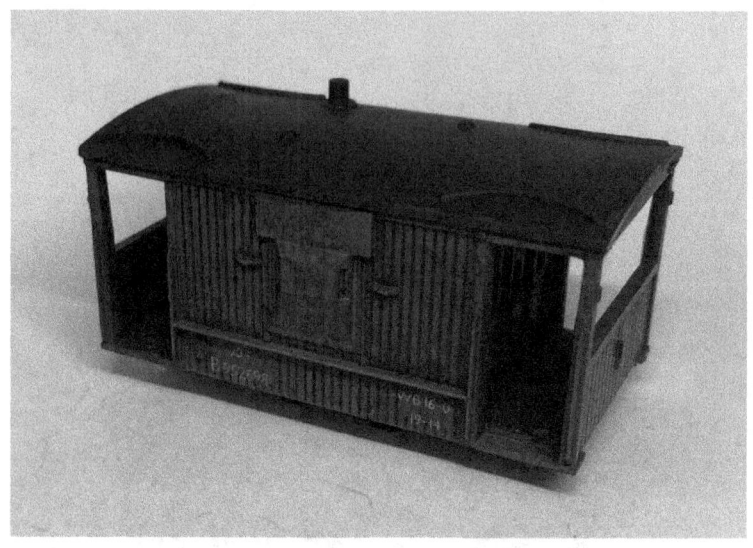

**Step 5**

At this stage, the wagon ironwork can also be picked out using white acrylic paint and a 5/0 or 10/0 brush.

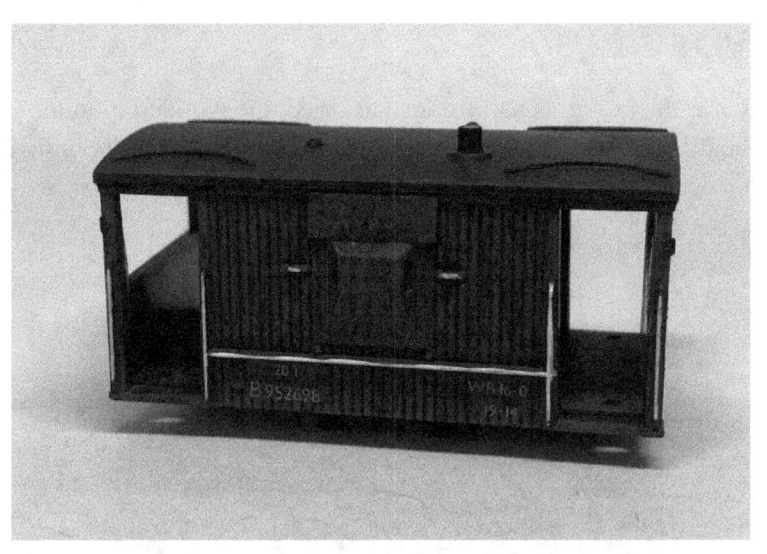

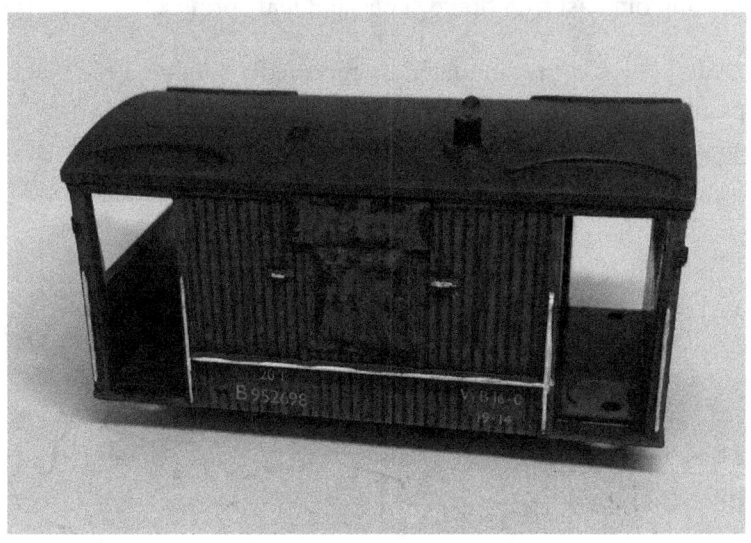

73

**Step 6**

Once the previous paint stage has dried, the wooden running boards can be accentuated from the black chassis by applying an acrylic wash (similar to Step 1) using a mixture of Burnt Umber acrylic paint and tap water.

Leave to dry fully.

**Step 7**

Now we will follow with hand painting rusty paint chips onto the chassis and ironwork using a 5/0 or 10/0 brush.

The wheels are painted in rust colour using a 2/0 brush, picking out cast iron brake shoes and leaf springs.

Deck plate wear is simulated by repeatedly sponging the black painted surface with rust coloured acrylic paint. Ensure the sponge is not too heavily loaded with paint prior to applying to the deck plate.

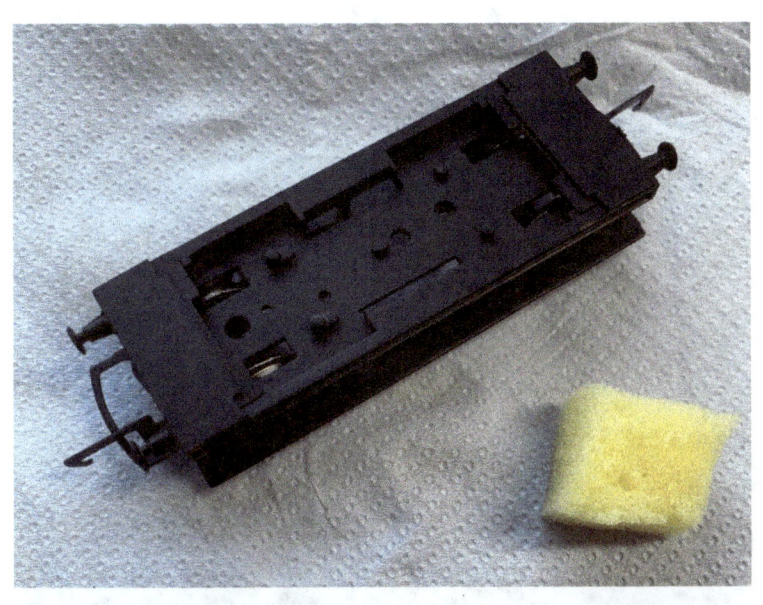

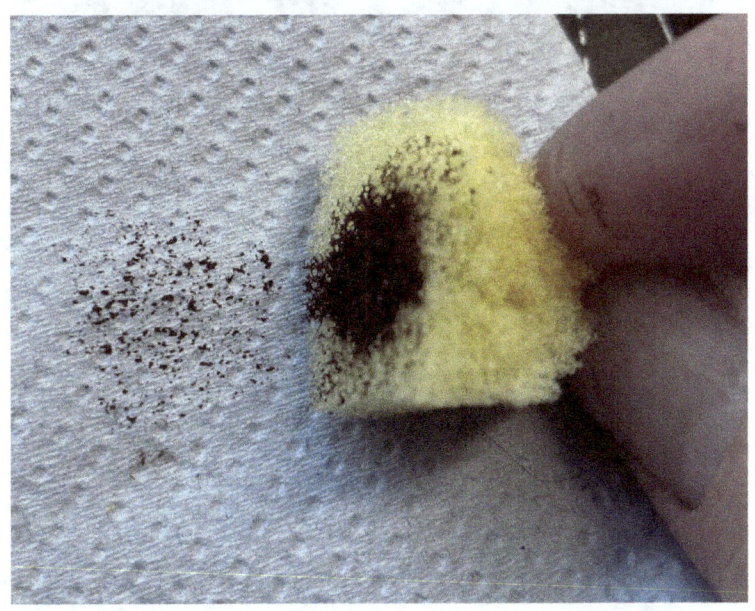

75

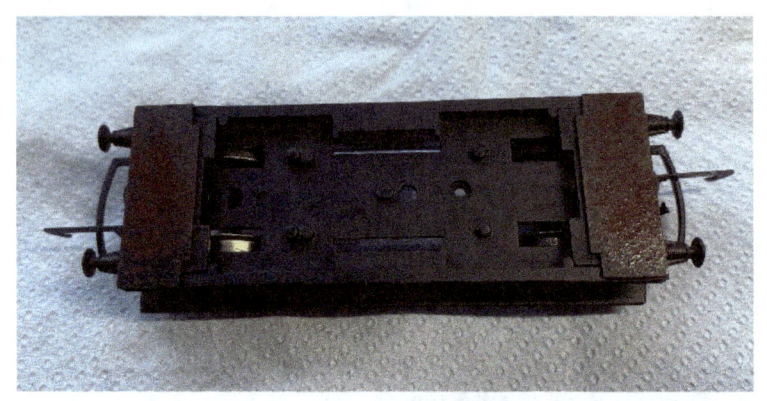

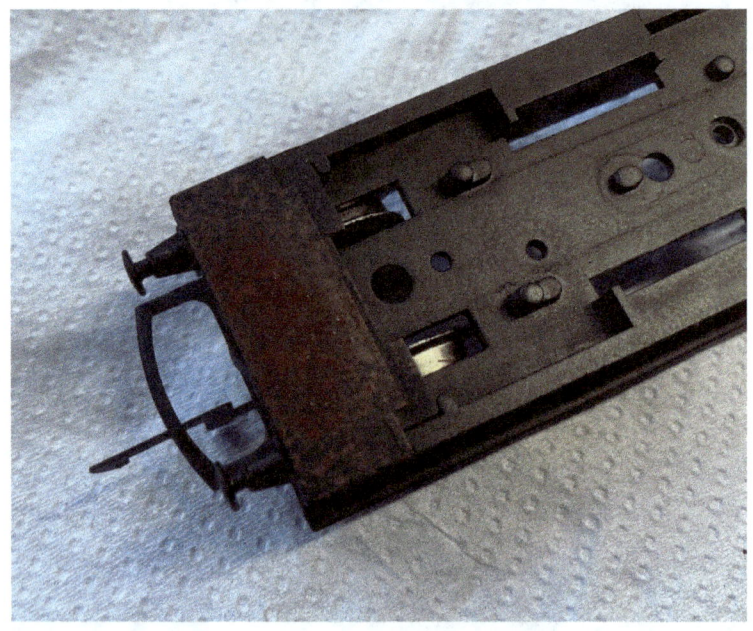

## Step 8

The final painting stage is picking out the buffer shafts in our silver acrylic colour using a 5/0 or 10/0 brush.

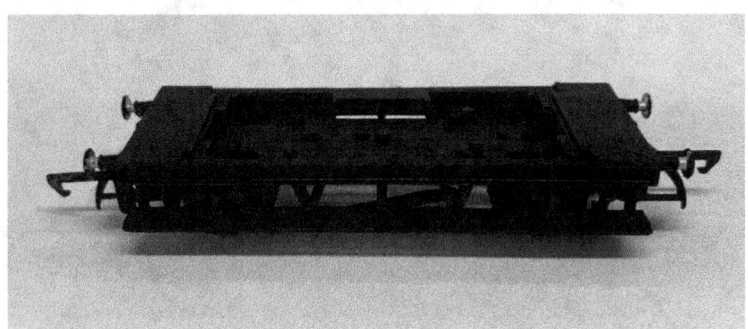

## Step 9

Once the acrylic paint is fully dry, we will apply a coat of satin acrylic varnish as a barrier layer using the airbrush.

Allow the varnish to fully cure for 24 hours to provide full protection of the paintwork below.

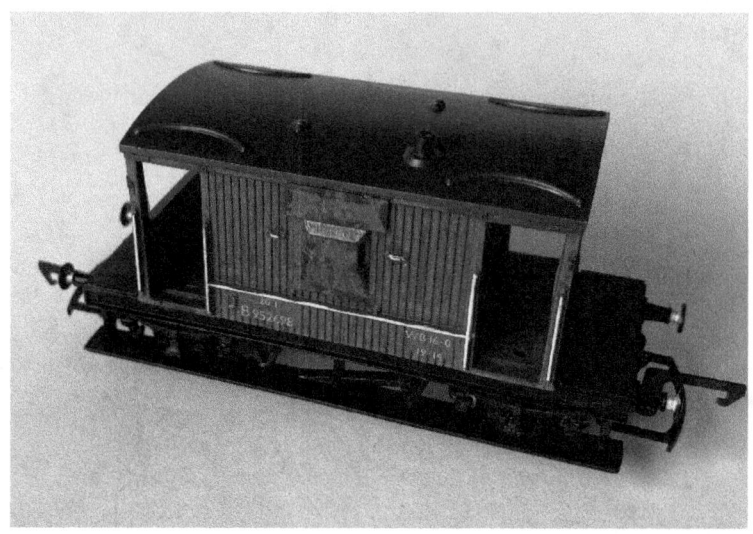

**Step 10**

To produce a less monolithic colour effect on the roof, we will apply a technique called a "dot filter" using our Oil Brushers. This technique is quite simple and with a little practice can produce an incredibly satisfying effect on wagon roofs.

First apply a few small dots of the dark brown oil paint along the upslope lines of the rain deflectors and around the roof vents and chimney. Next, apply a few random dots around the roof of the dark grey and medium grey oil paints.

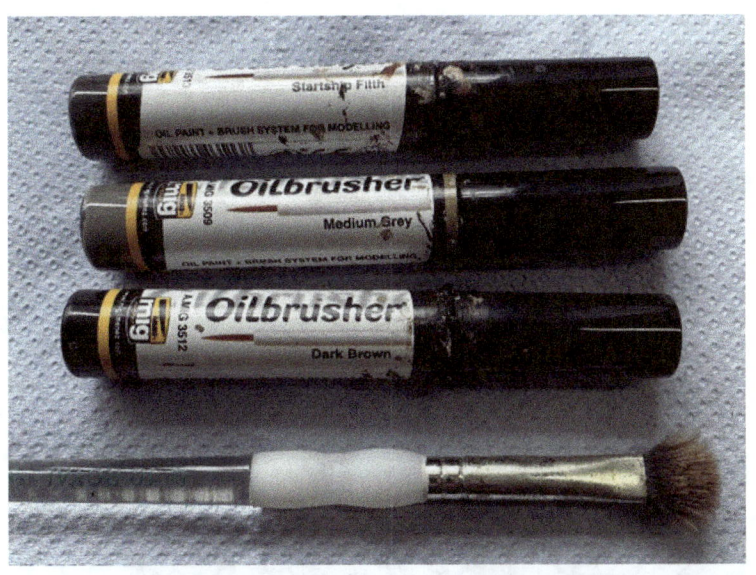

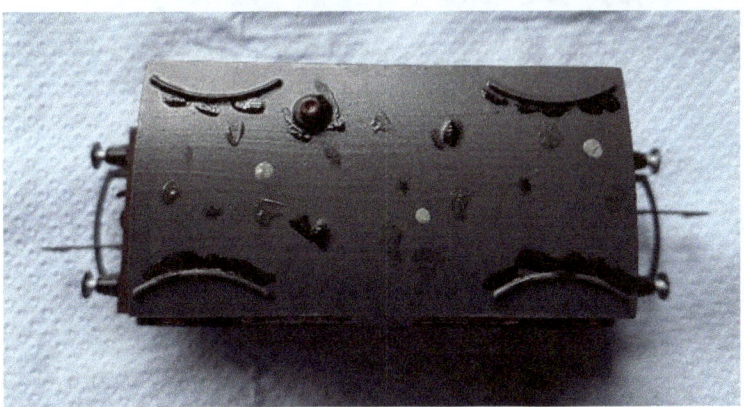

Moisten a Size 10 brush in enamel thinners and dry on a paper towel until no thinners is transferred to the towel.

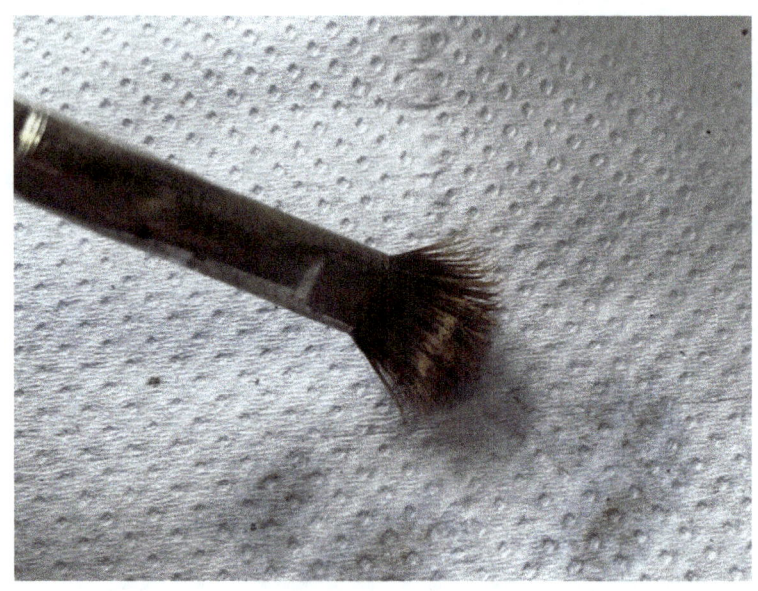

Using the brush, spread the dark brown oil paint around the roof protrusions and then wipe the brush on the paper towel.

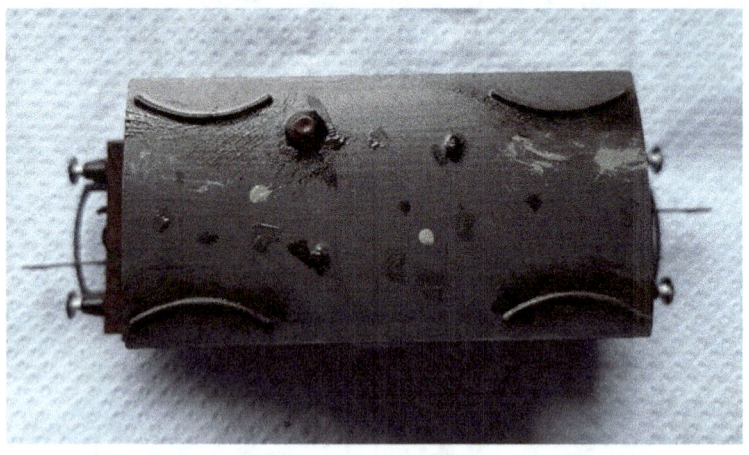

Starting from the centre line of the roof, use single brush strokes to drag streaks of the oil paints to the edge of the roof. Periodically wipe the brush on the paper towel. Repeat for the other side of the roof.

Repeat the single stroke streaking for both sides of the roof and wipe the brush on the paper towel.

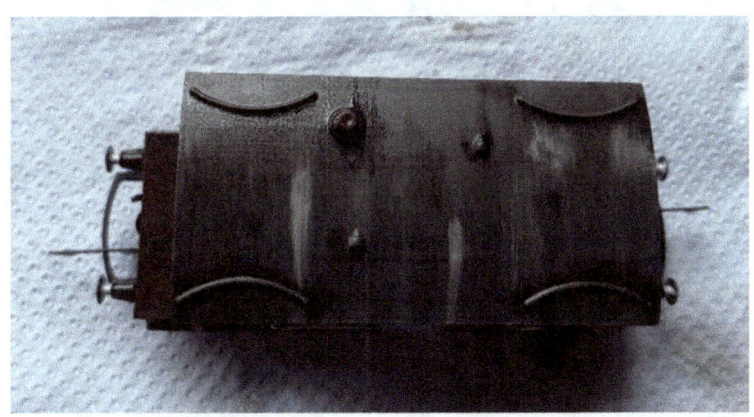

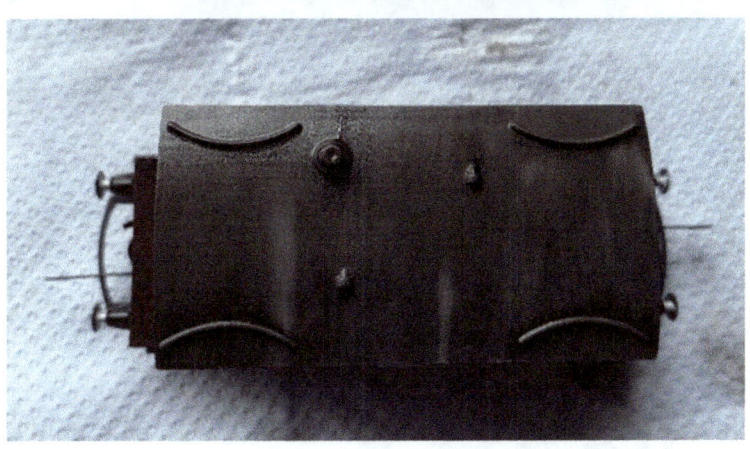

Finally, with a rapid two directional brush stroke action pass over the entire roof blurring the oil paint streaks.

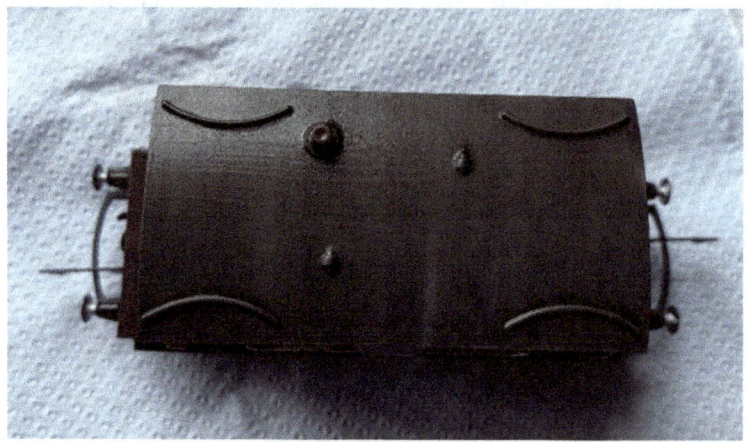

Leave to dry for 24 hours.

**Step 11**

We will now apply a suitably coloured enamel wash, as we are dealing with a brown painted wagon, a dark grey wash is used.

Using a 2/0 brush, apply the well shaken enamel wash to each raised or recessed detail on the wagon body and allow the wash to flow along the moulded edges.

Leave the wash to dry for around 30 minutes.

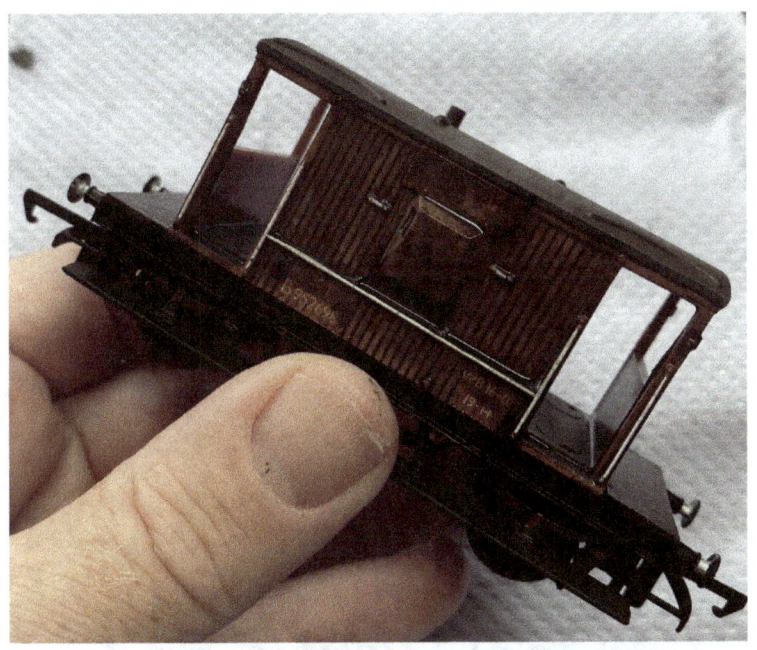

**Step 12**

Once the wash has dried sufficiently, as done in Chapter 3, remove the excess wash using a broad tipped size 10 brush moistened in odourless enamel thinners.

Leave to dry for 24 hours.

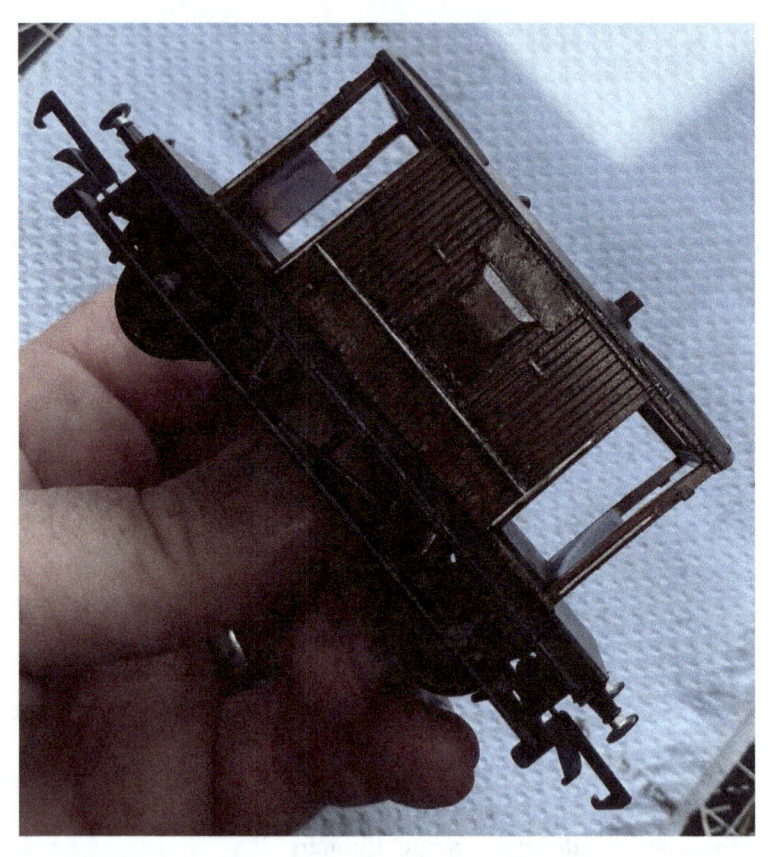

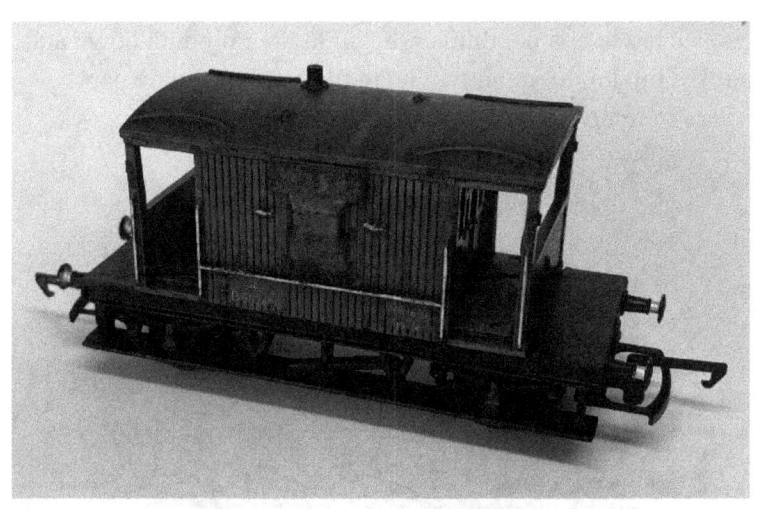

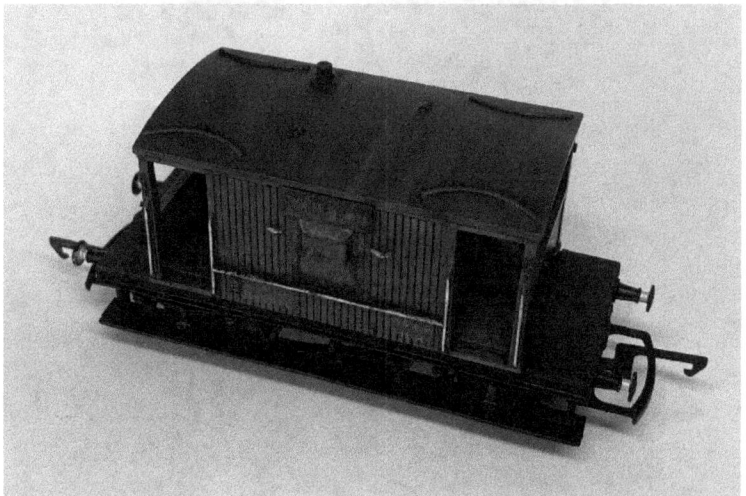

**Step 13**

Create the dirt streaks down the walls from the rain deflectors, using the dark brown oil paint. Then, using a 2/0 round brush moistened in enamel thinner, begin to drag product down and off the model. Frequently wiping the brush on some paper towel to removed excess oil paint.

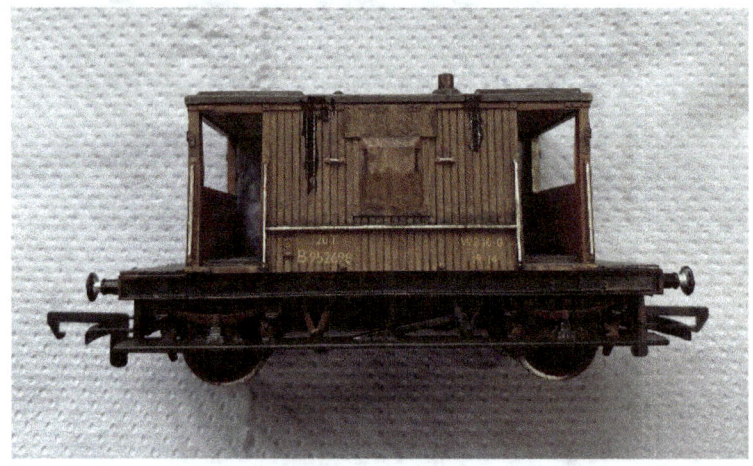

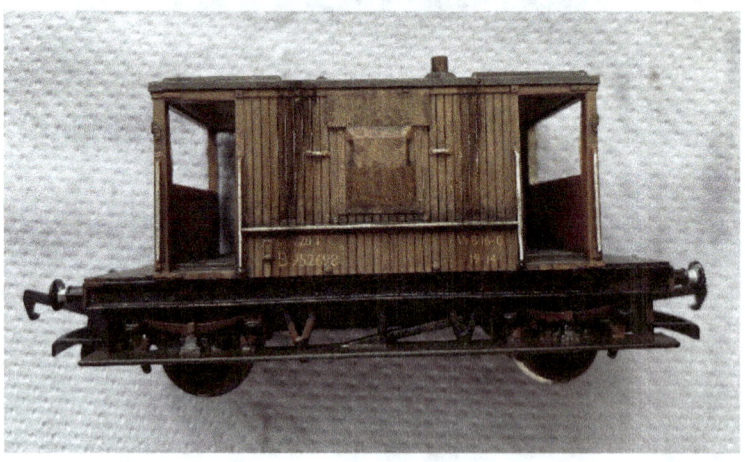

**Step 14**

Use the airbrush to apply a misted coat of our chosen dirt colour to the chassis and lower regions of the wagon body.

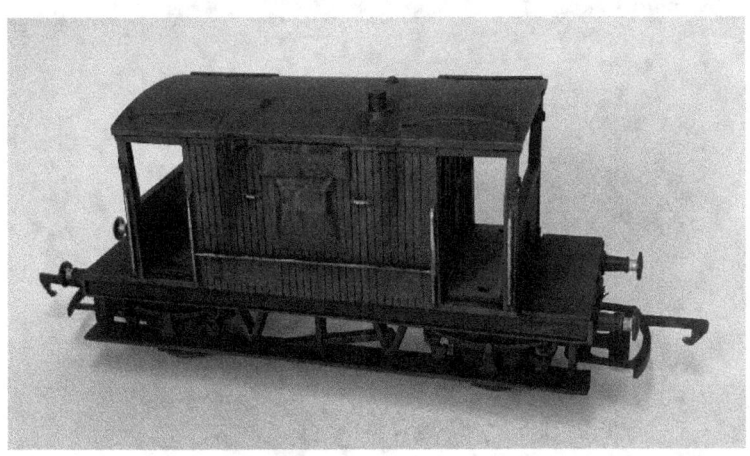

**Step 15**

Apply two coats of matt acrylic varnish using the airbrush.

**Step 16**

Add oil and grease effects on the buffer ends and axle bearing boxes, applied using a 5/0 brush and our chosen oil effect product.

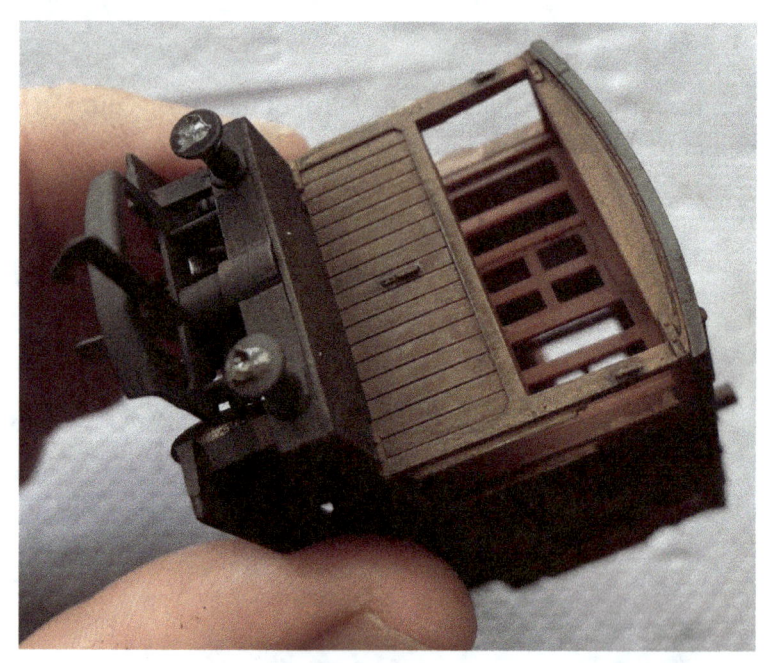

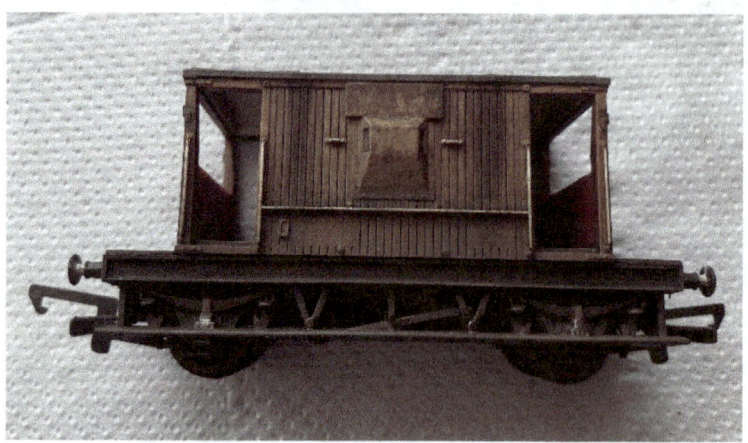

Leave the oil effects to dry fully.

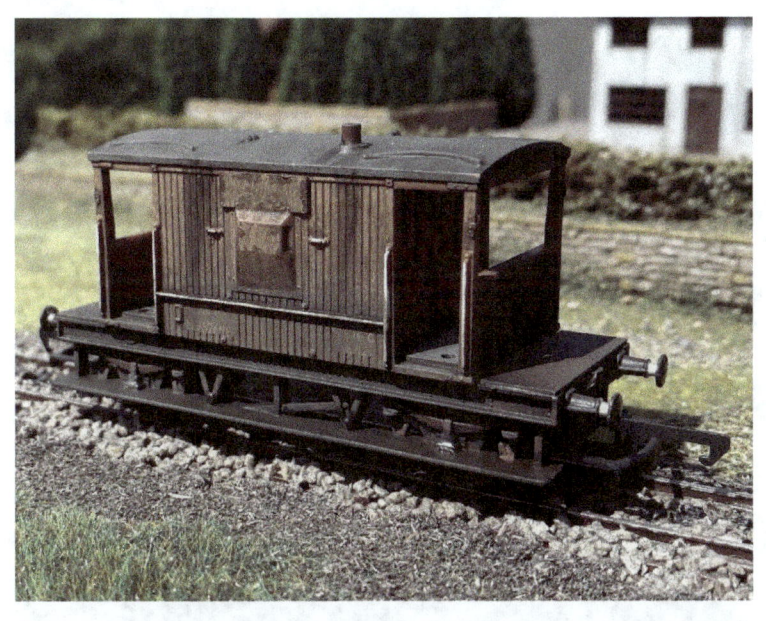

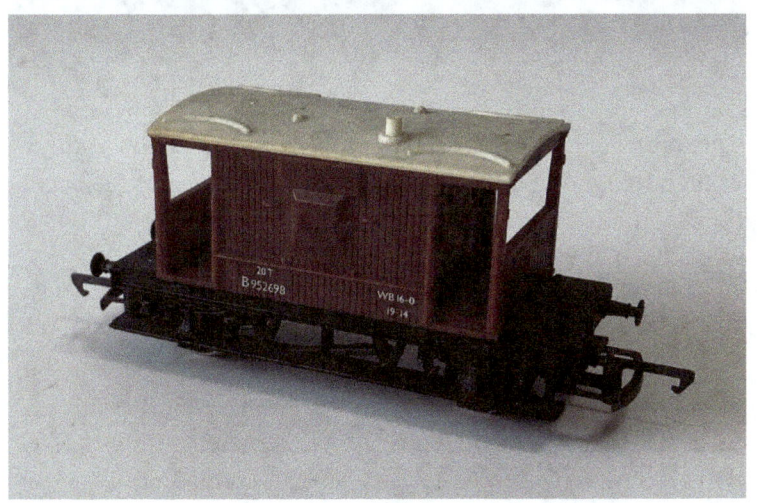

# Chapter 7 –Hornby 21t Mineral Wagon (meths fading and weathering)

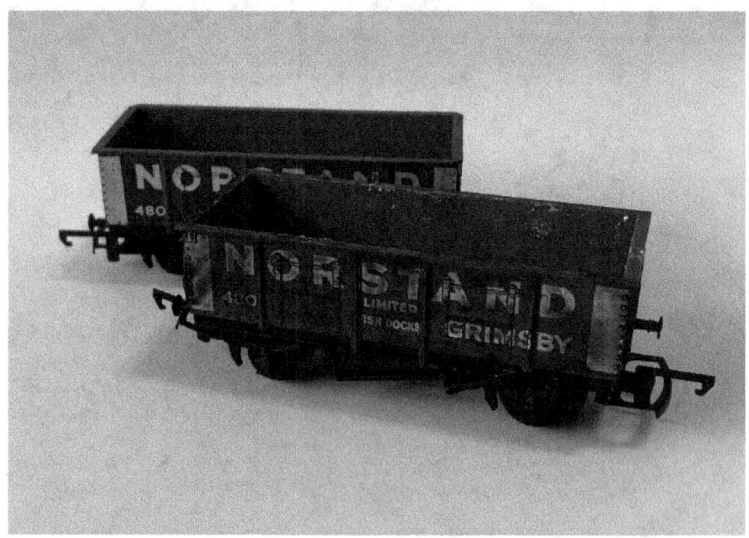

This project is based on a Hornby 21t mineral wagon with printed livery on bare plastic in order to demonstrate effects for steel body wagons and fading of printed detail.

The examples I used for this project had both been messed around with at some point in the past, one having a now yellowed coat of gloss varnish and the other having been given some sort of rudimentary black weathering. In both cases, the use of methylated spirit will lessen the impact of these old treatments.

As usual, before starting the painting process, the wagon will get a scrub in water and washing up liquid, followed by a thorough rinse and left to air dry for a day. Again, the body can be carefully prised from the chassis to be dealt with separately.

In addition to the equipment listed in Chapter 2, for this project you will require the following items or suitable equivalents:

| Item | What I used |
|---|---|
| Black acrylic primer | Mig Ammo One Shot Primer, Black |
| Acrylic paint | Mig Ammo, Old Rust |
| Acrylic paint | Mig Ammo, White |
| Acrylic paint | Mig Ammo, Matt Aluminium |
| Acrylic paint | Rail Match, Frame Dirt |
| Acrylic varnish, satin | Mig Ammo Lucky Varnish |
| Acrylic varnish, matt | Winsor & Newton Galleria |
| Enamel wash | Mig Ammo, Starship Wash |
| Oil effect | Mig Ammo, Fresh Engine Oil |
| Solvent | Methylated Spirit |
| Solvent applicator | Nylon scouring pad |
| Size 4 brush | |
| Size 5/0 brush | |
| Size 10/0 brush | |
| Size 2/0 brush | |
| Size 10 brush | |

## Step 1

In order to dull the sheen of the plastic body and simulate weather fading of painted livery details, we will attack the wagon body with a nylon scouring pad wetted with methylated spirits.

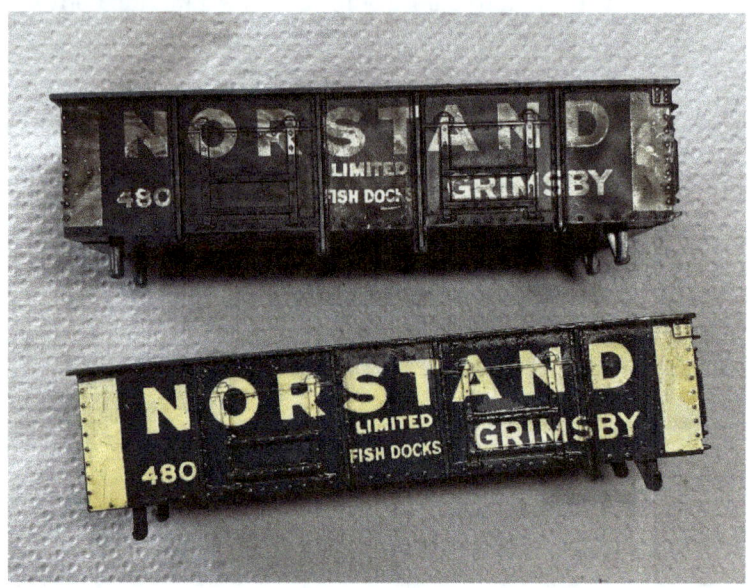

Obviously, this is quite an aggressive solvent so protective gloves and safety glasses should be worn for this stage. Likewise, it should be undertaken in a well-ventilated area, preferably outdoors.

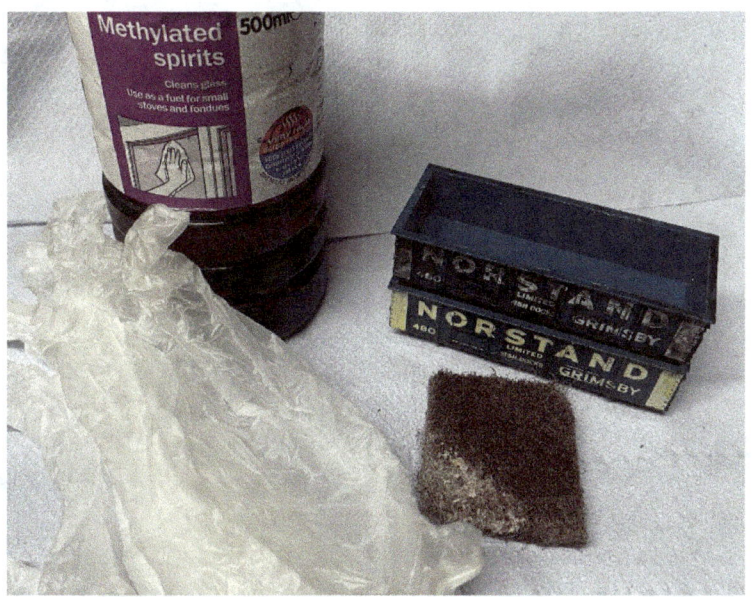

First, lightly wet the wagon sides with methylated spirits on the scouring pad and allow the spirit to attack the surface for a few seconds.

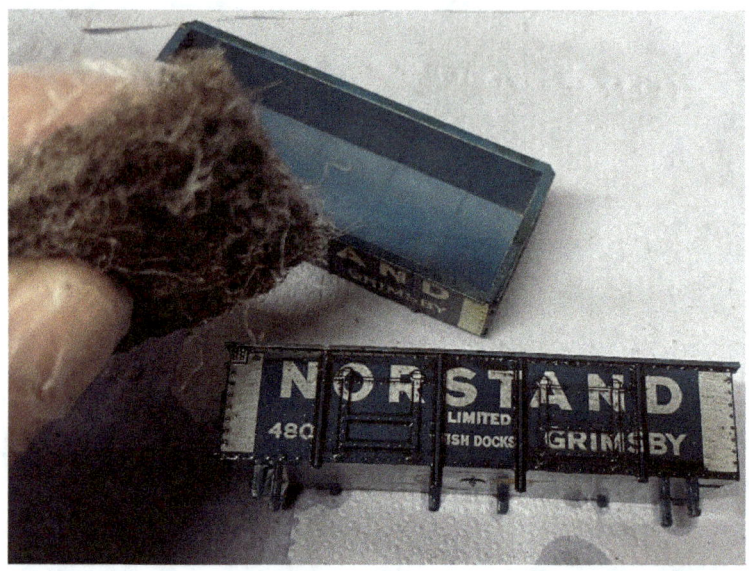

Next, lightly rub the wagon sides with the spirit wetted scouring pad until the desired degree of fading of the painted detail has been achieved.

Wipe the wagon dry with paper towel to remove paint residue before the spirit fully evaporates from the wagon.

The wagon body can be rinsed in clean water and left to dry at this stage.

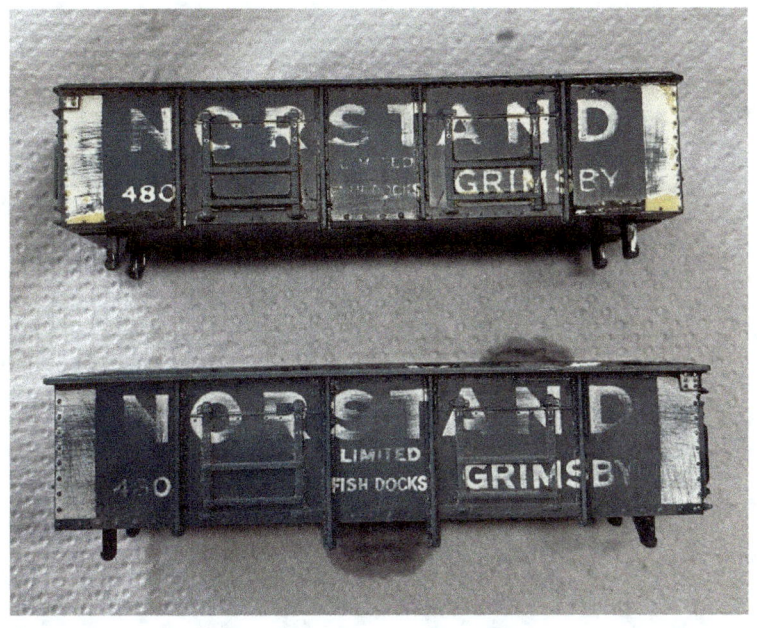

**Step 2**

Once the wagon is dry, the wagon interior is hand painted
with a black acrylic primer using a size 4 brush.

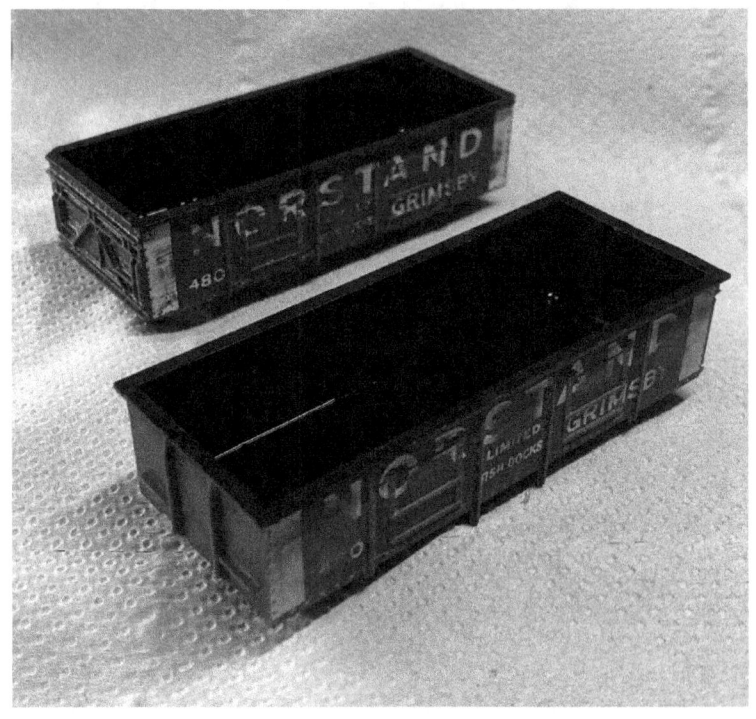

## Step 3

The chassis can now be airbrushed with black acrylic primer
or spray painted with acrylic matt black.

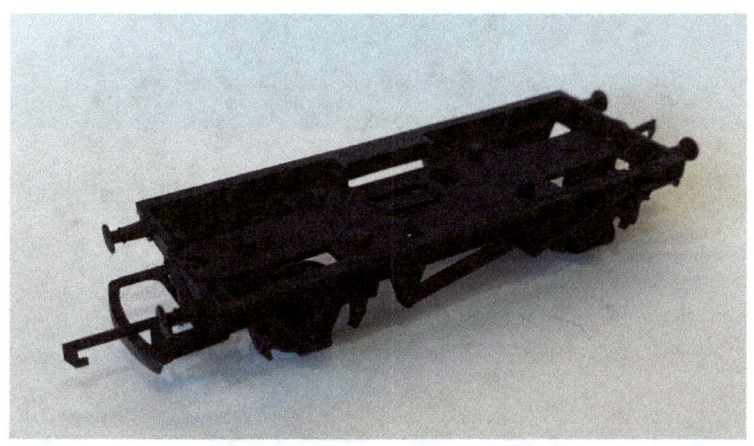

**Step 4**

Once the primer is dry, the interior is sponged with rust colour acrylic paint to simulate wear (do not sponge into the corners, the exposed black primer will create an effect of accumulated coal dust)

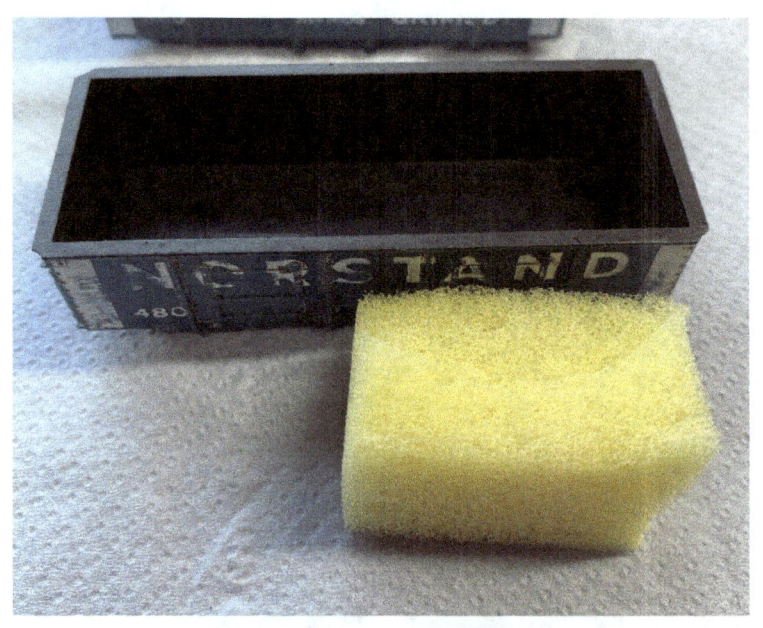

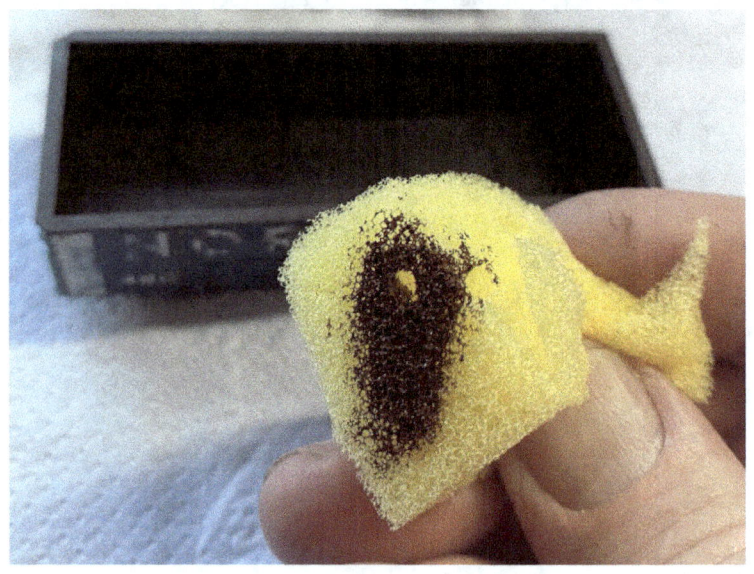

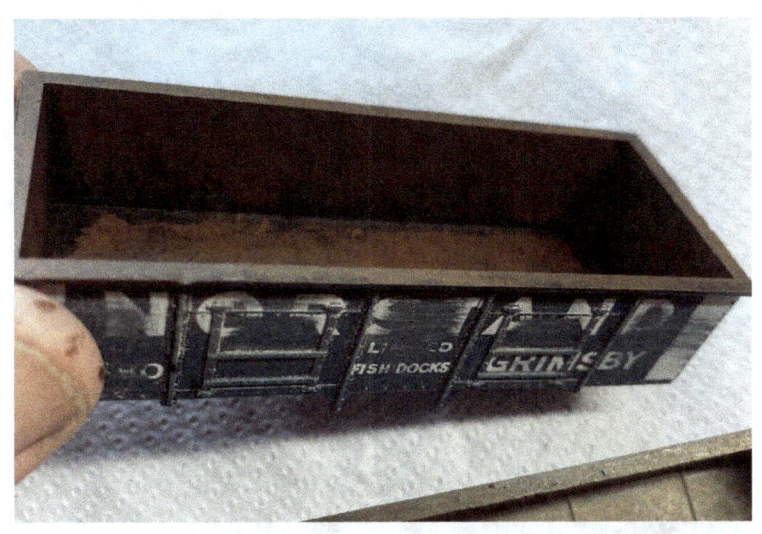

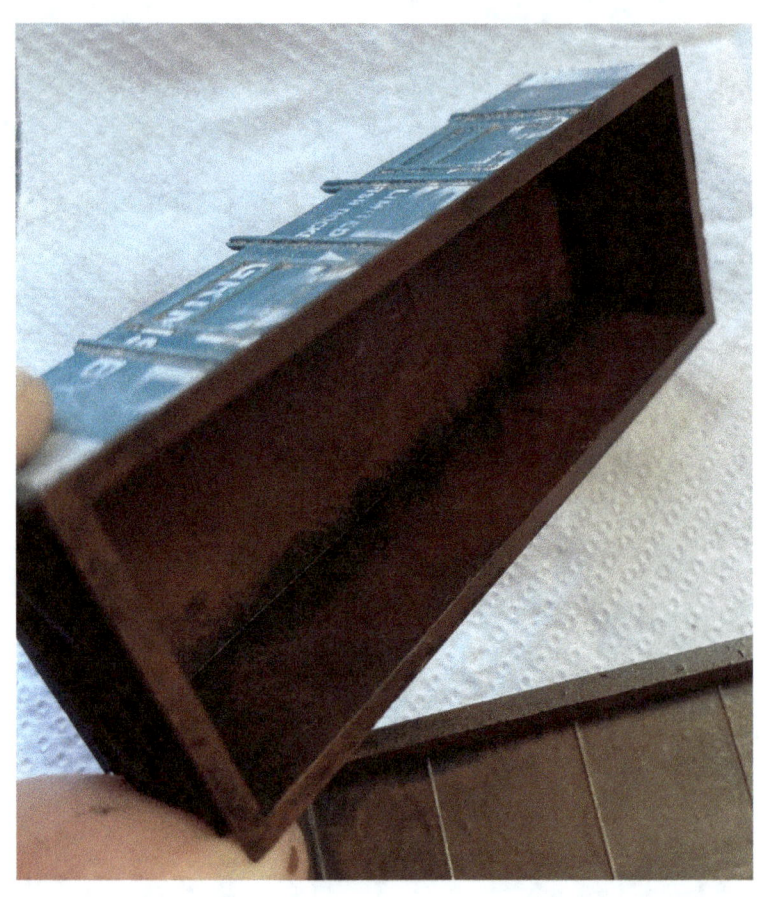

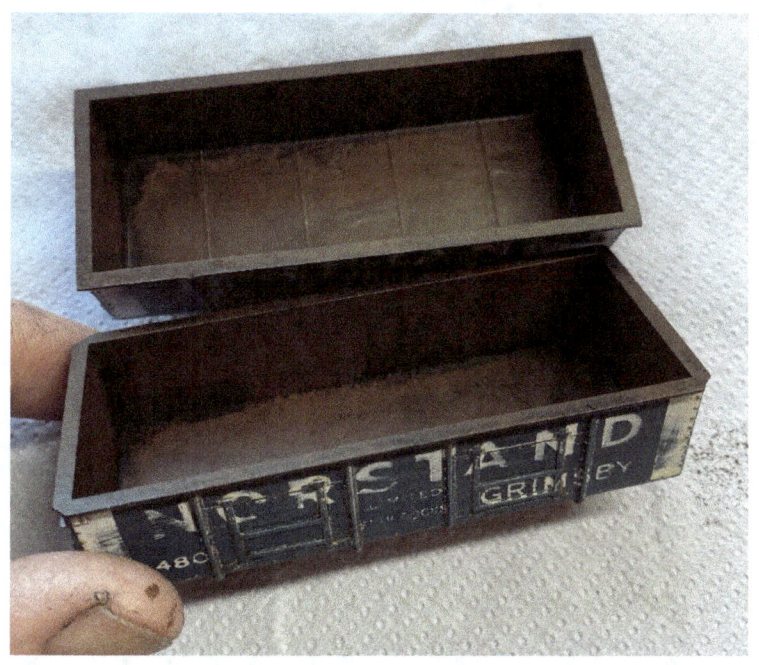

**Step 5**

Now we will hand paint rusty paint chips onto the chassis and body ribs using a small section of sponge held in tweezers.

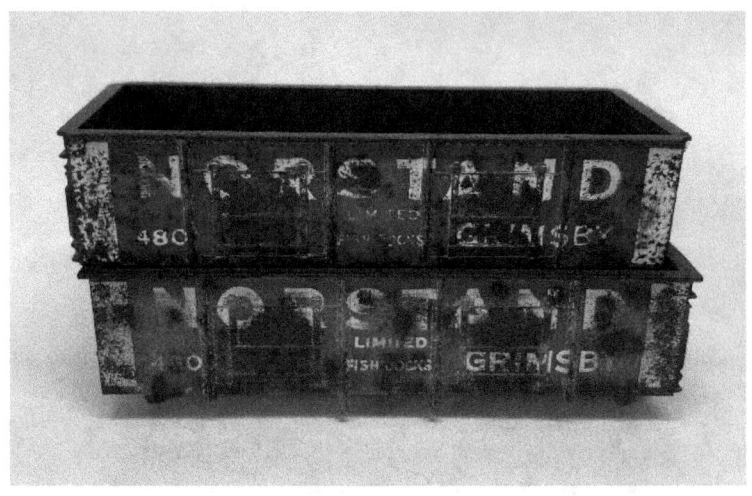

## Step 5

The wheels are painted in rust colour using a 2/0 brush, picking out cast iron brake shoes and leaf springs.

The final painting stage is picking out the buffer shafts in our silver acrylic colour and handbrake lever handles in white acrylic using a 5/0 or 10/0 brush.

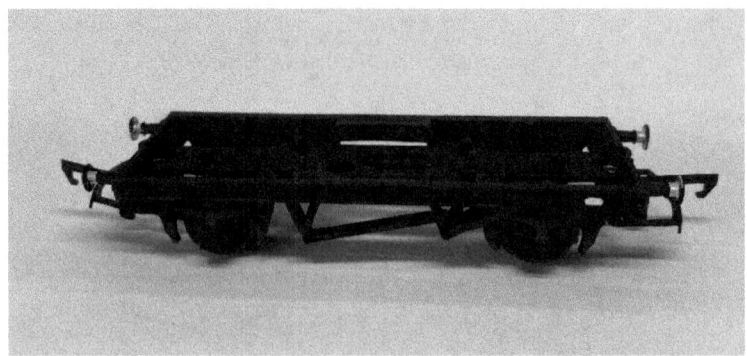

The model can then be reassembled.

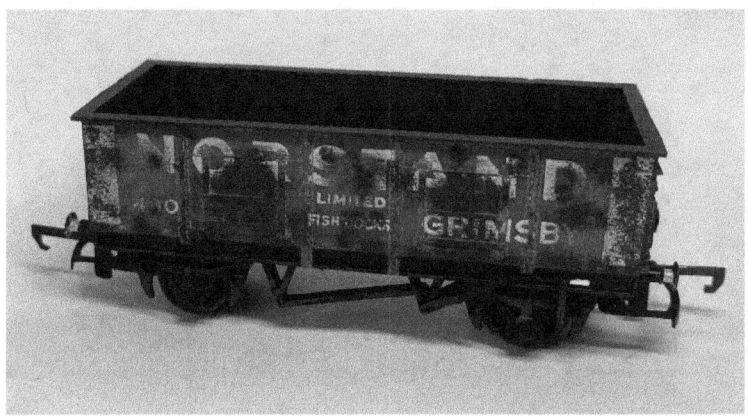

**Step 6**

Once the acrylic paint is fully dry, apply a coat of satin acrylic varnish as a barrier layer using the airbrush.

Allow the varnish to fully cure for 24 hours to provide full protection of the paintwork below.

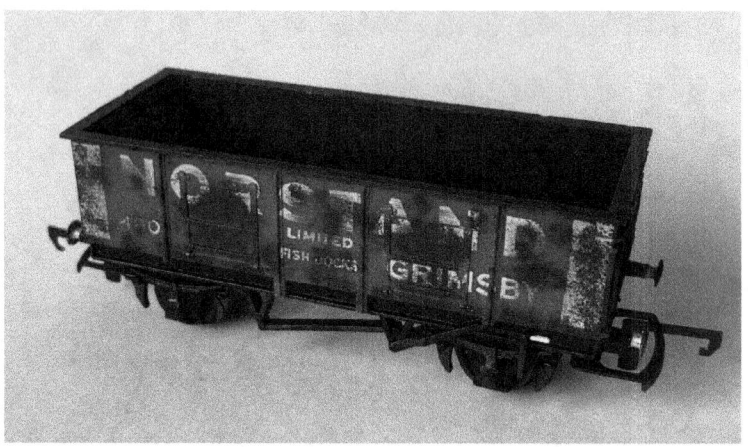

**Step 7**

Now apply a suitably coloured enamel wash, as this is a coal wagon, a dark coloured wash is most appropriate.

Using a 2/0 brush, apply the well shaken enamel wash to each raised or recessed detail on the wagon body and allow the wash to flow along the moulded edges.

Leave the wash to dry for around 30 minutes. One hint here, for steel bodied wagons, I leave the body to dry upside down so that the wash accumulates under the top lip (this will provide helpful effects later).

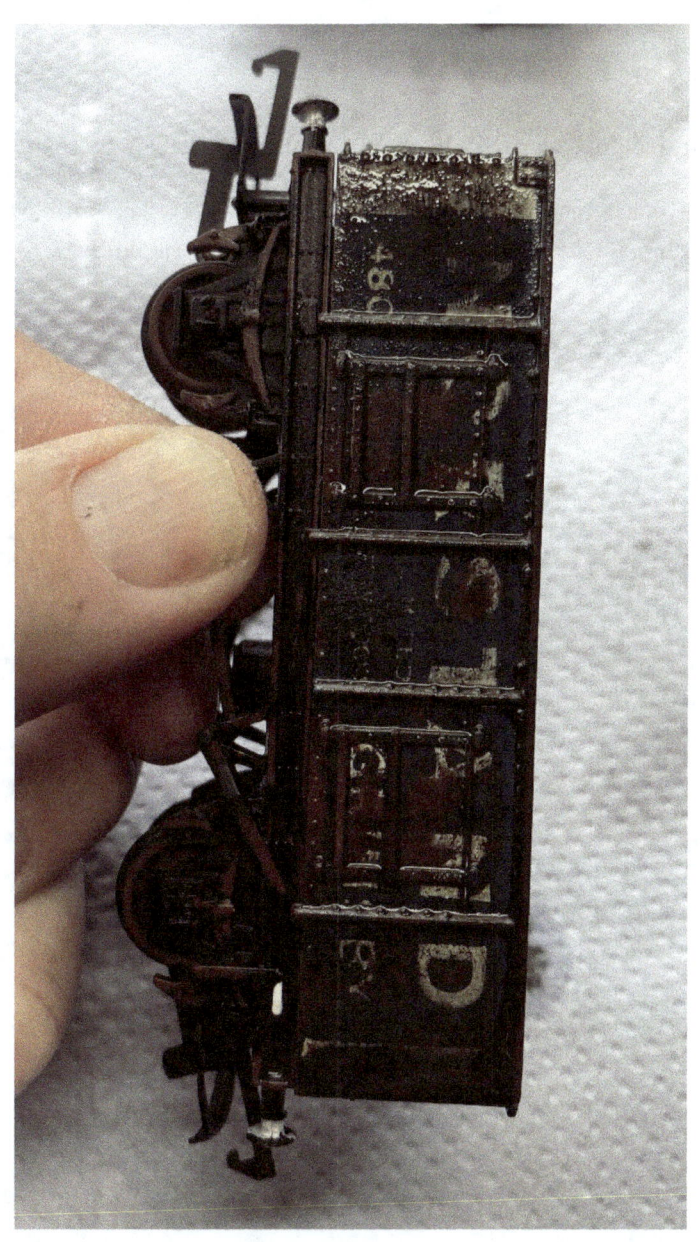

**Step 8**

Once the wash has dried sufficiently, as done in Chapter 4, remove the excess wash using a broad tipped size 10 brush.

Work, as always, in vertical downward strokes. This will draw wash deposits from below the top rim across the body as streaks.

Leave to dry for 24 hours.

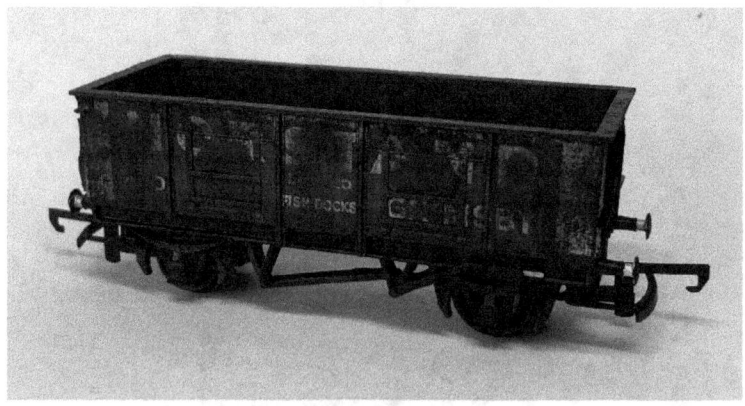

**Step 9**

Use the airbrush to apply a misted coat of our chosen dirt colour to the chassis and lower regions of the wagon body.

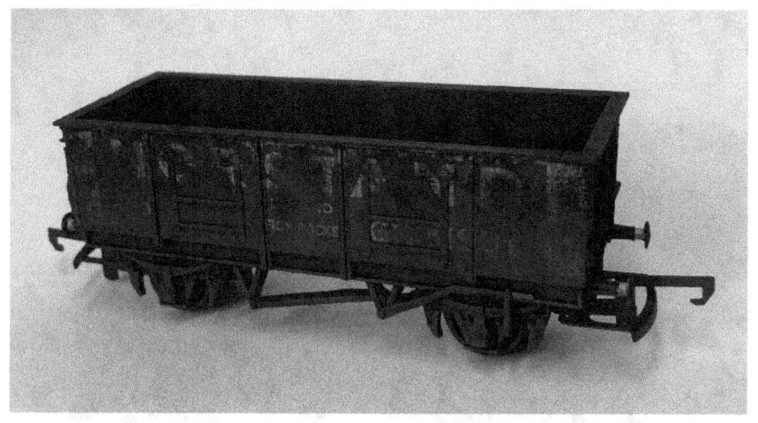

## Step 10

Apply two coats of matt acrylic varnish using the airbrush.

## Step 11

Add oil and grease effects on the buffer ends and axle bearing boxes, applied using a 5/0 brush and our chosen oil effect product.

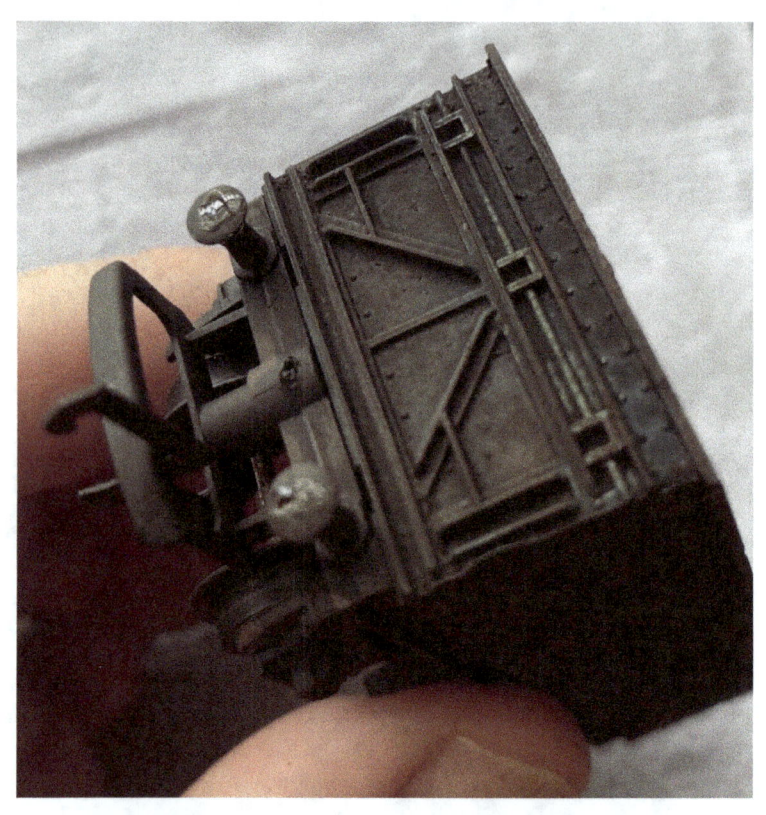

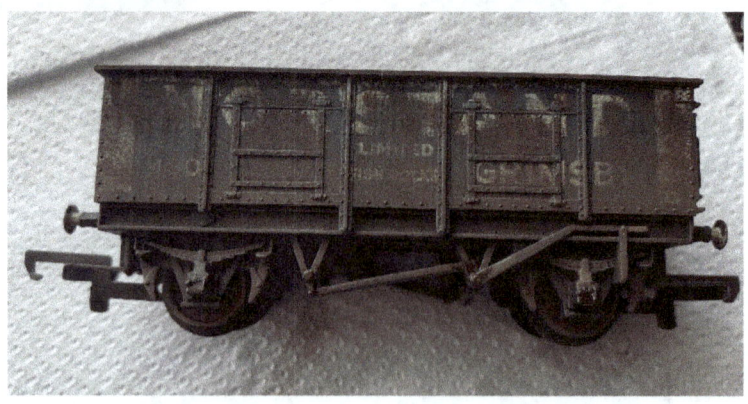

Leave the oil effects to fully dry.

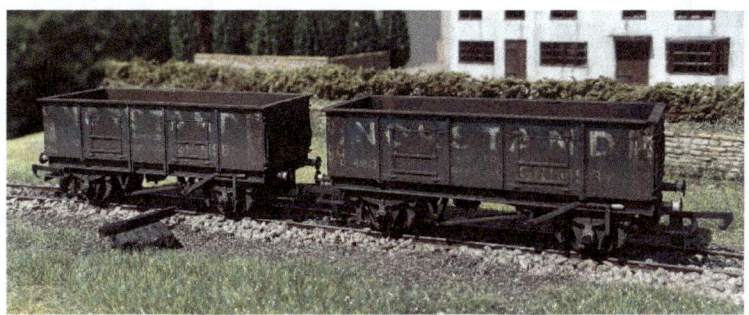

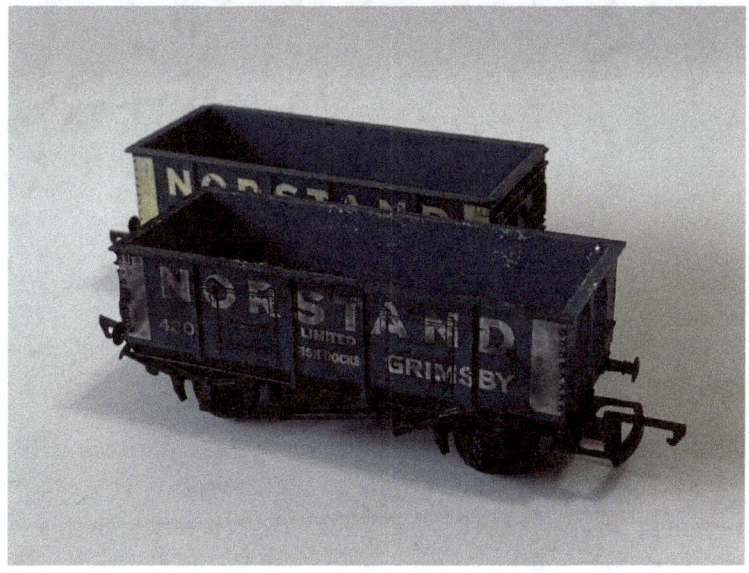

## Chapter 8 – Triang Plank Wagon (black primer, repaint & weathering)

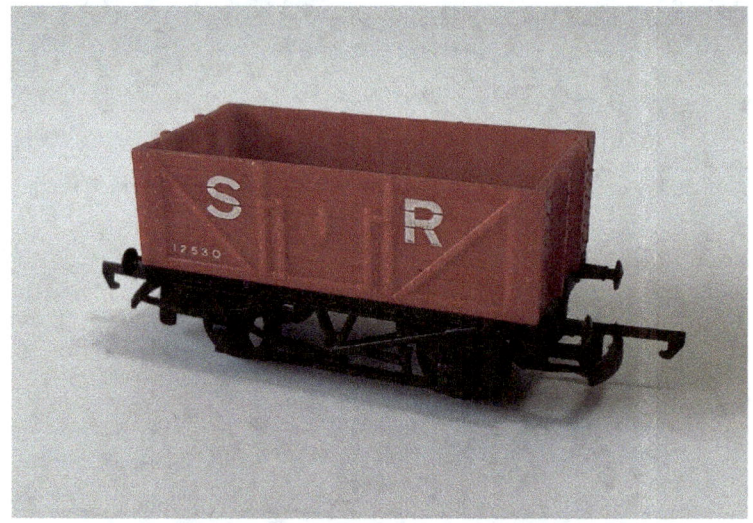

In this project, we will be working on a Triang plank wagon, a rather plain looking item from the 1960s or early 1970s.

As usual, before starting the painting process, the wagon will get a scrub in water and washing up liquid, followed by a thorough rinse and left to air dry for a day. However, in this case, the body must be carefully prised from the chassis prior to painting to be dealt with separately. You may find it more convenient to separate the body and chassis prior to cleaning (see Step 1).

In addition to the equipment listed in Chapter 2, for this project you will require the following items or suitable equivalents.

| Item | What I used |
|---|---|
| Black acrylic primer | Halfords aerosol, matt black |
| Acrylic paint | Mig Ammo, Stone Grey |
| Acrylic paint | Mig Ammo, Old Rust |
| Acrylic paint | Mig Ammo, White |
| Acrylic paint | Mig Ammo, Matt Aluminium |
| Acrylic paint | Rail Match, Frame Dirt |
| Acrylic varnish, satin | Mig Ammo Lucky Varnish |
| Acrylic varnish, matt | Winsor & Newton Galleria |
| Enamel wash | Mig Ammo, Starship Wash |
| Oil effect | Mig Ammo, Fresh Engine Oil |
| Size 4 brush | |
| Size 5/0 brush | |
| Size 10/0 brush | |
| Size 2/0 brush | |
| Size 10 brush | |

**Step 1**

As this project will involve repainting of the wagon body, it is easiest to conduct this after removing the wagon from the chassis. Triang and Hornby wagon bodies secured by means of the four melted posts in the floor corners can be carefully levered away from the chassis using a small screwdriver.

Once removed, if the post ends are burred over, they can be trimmed off using a sprue cutter. Likewise, floor holes can be cleared out using a small drill bit to aid reassembly.

**Step 2**

Once separated from each other, the wagon body is sprayed with a black acrylic primer using the airbrush or an aerosol can of acrylic matt black (I have found that standard acrylic car spray paint bonds satisfactorily to models).

It is also worthwhile giving the chassis a coat of black primer or matt black while it is separated.

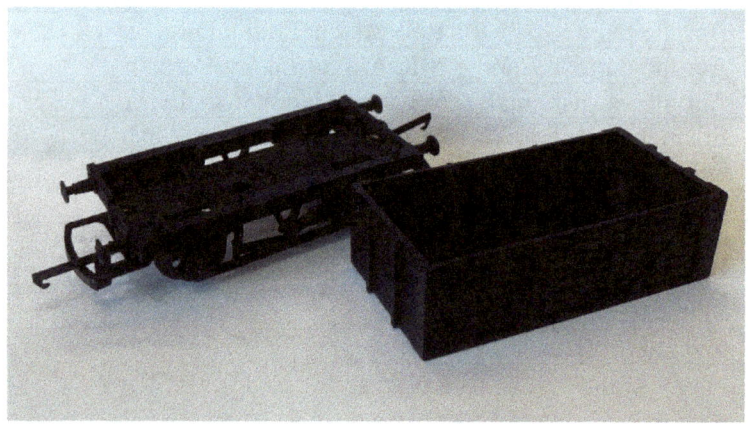

**Step 3**

Once the primer is dry, the wagon body exterior is painted with the Stone Grey using the airbrush. Do not coat too heavily, allow the black primer to show through at the plank joints.

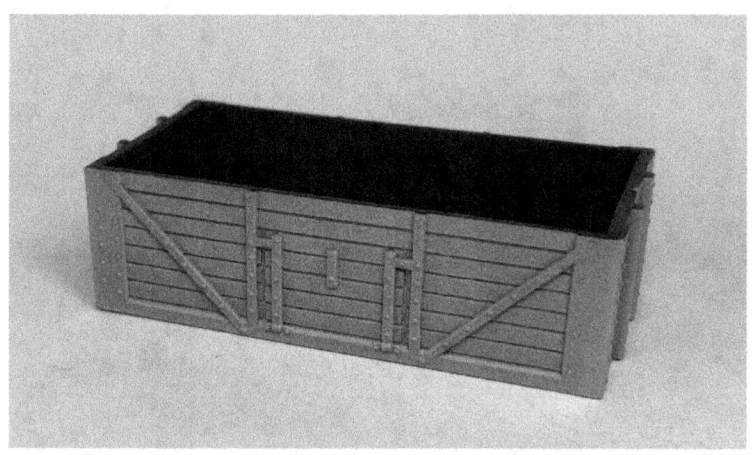

**Step 4**

Once the grey acrylic is dry, we can pick out some details on the wagon body using a 5/0 or 10/0 brush:

- Diagonal braces on one end (both sides) picked out in white acrylic.
- Small rectangles at each end picked out in matt black acrylic.

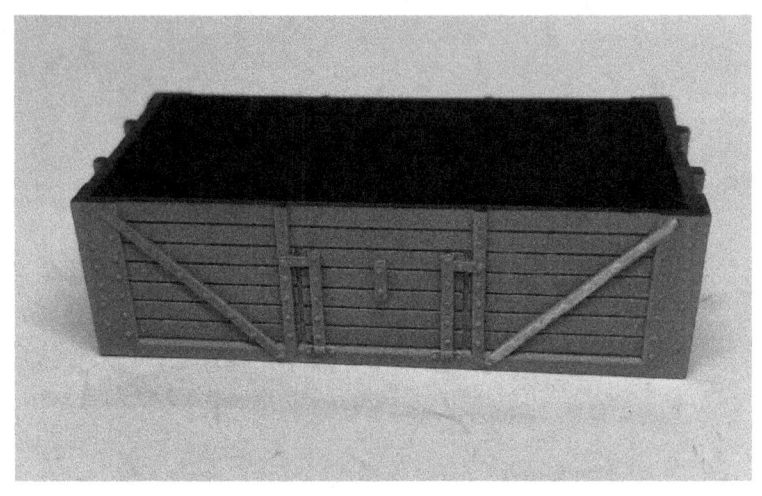

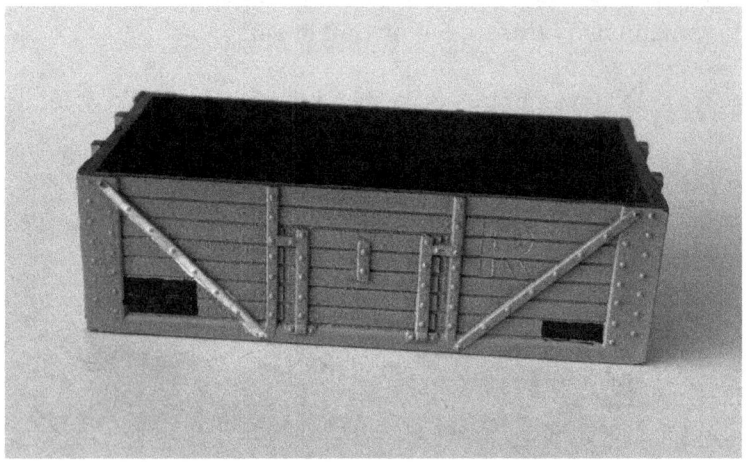

**Step 5**

This is followed by hand painting rusty paint chips onto the
chassis and ironwork using a 5/0 or 10/0 brush.

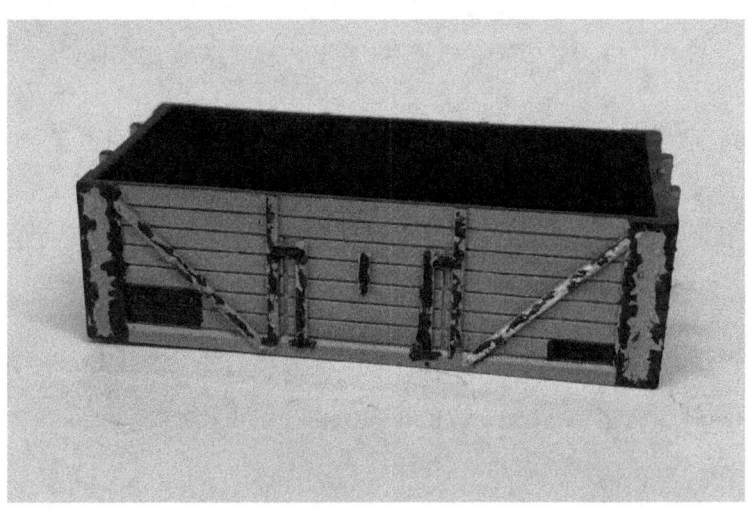

## Step 6

The wheels are painted in rust colour using a 2/0 brush. Picking out cast iron brake shoes and leaf springs with the rust colour.

## Step 7

The final painting stage involves picking out the buffer shafts in our silver acrylic colour and the brake lever handles and one diagonal brace on each side using white acrylic using a 5/0 or 10/0 brush.

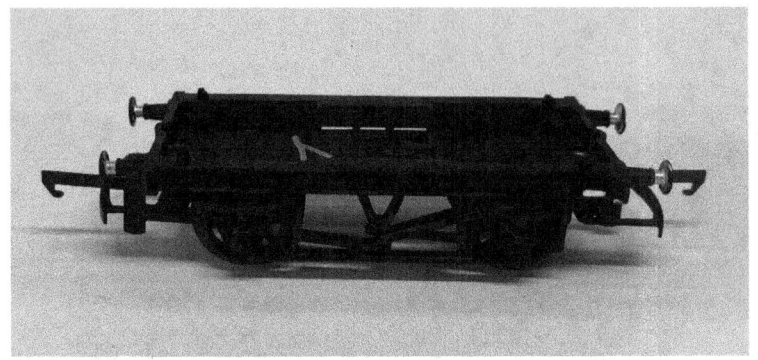

**Step 8**

Once dry, the wagon can now be reassembled.

A dab of rubberised superglue around each post will secure the body in position after test fitting prior to glue application.

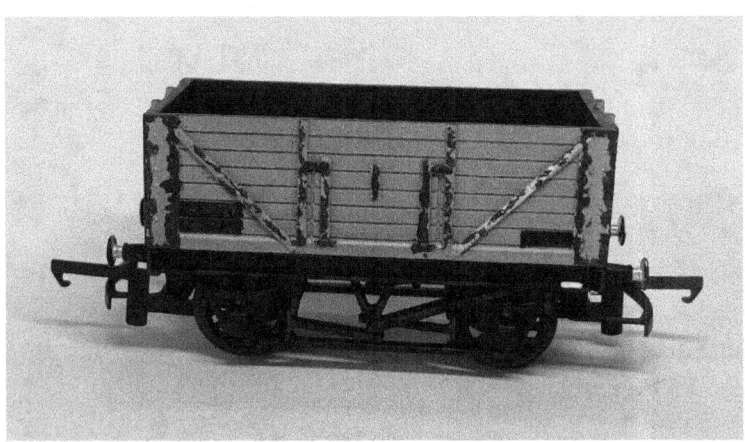

**Step 9**

Once the acrylic paint is fully dry, apply a coat of satin acrylic varnish using the airbrush.

Allow the varnish to fully cure for 24 hours.

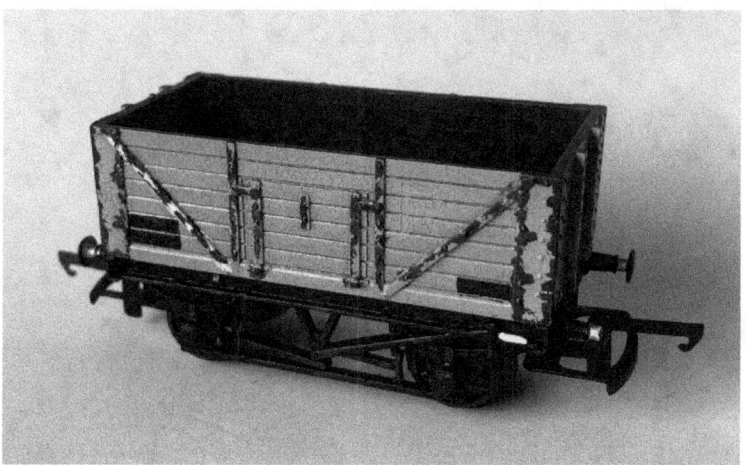

**Step 10**

Using a 2/0 brush, apply the well shaken enamel wash to each raised or recessed detail on the wagon body and allow the wash to flow along the moulded edges.

Leave the wash to dry for around 30 minutes.

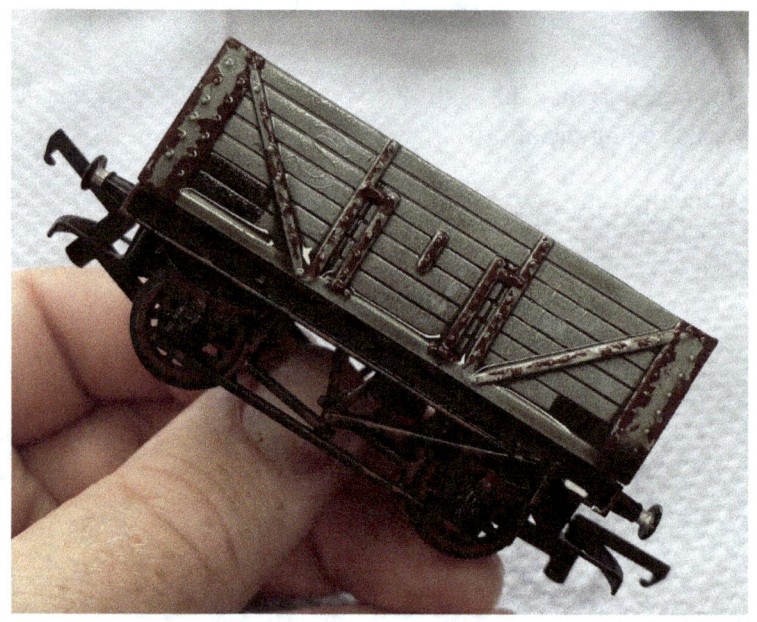

**Step 11**

Once the wash has dried sufficiently, remove the excess wash using a broad tipped size 10 brush moistened in odourless enamel thinners.

Leave to dry for 24 hours.

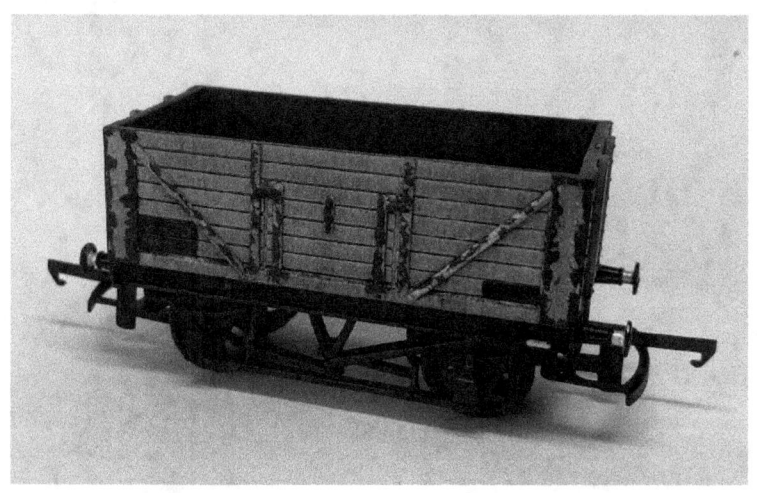

**Step 12**

Create the dirt streaks down the walls, using the dark brown
oil paint. Then, using a 2/0 round brush moistened in enamel
thinner, begin to drag product down and off the model.
Frequently wiping the brush on some paper towel to removed
excess oil paint.

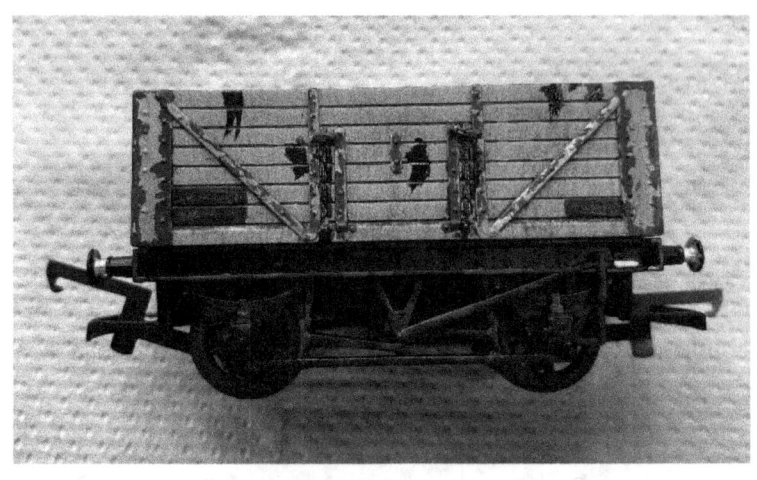

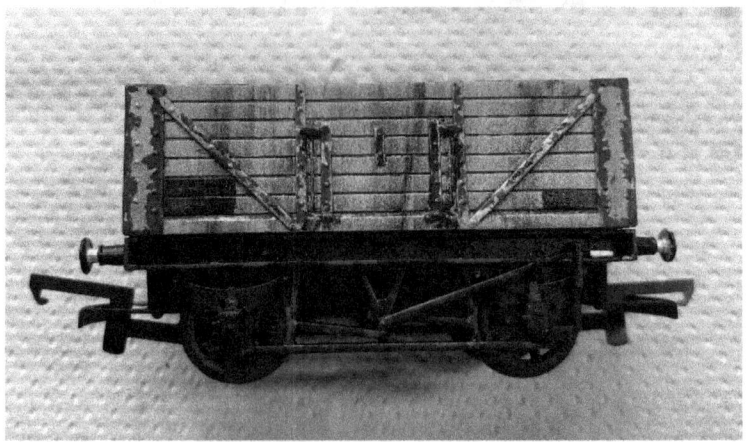

**Step 13**

Use the airbrush to apply a misted coat of our chosen dirt colour to the chassis and lower regions of the wagon body and body ends.

120

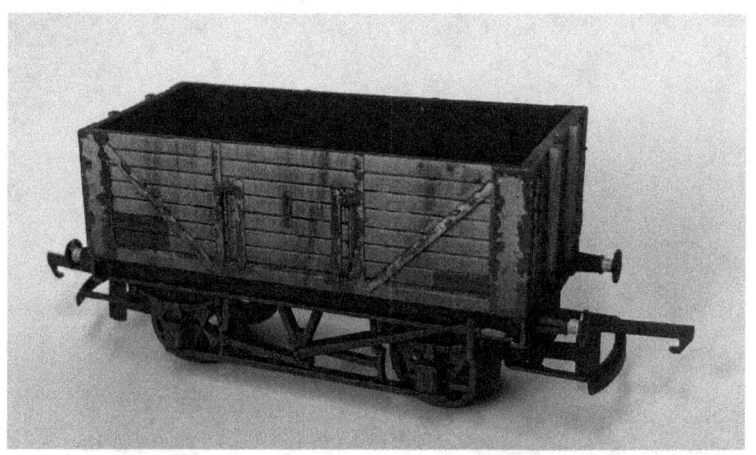

**Step 14**

Apply two coats of matt acrylic varnish using the airbrush.

**Step 15**

Add oil and grease effects on the buffer ends and axle bearing boxes, applied using a 5/0 brush and our chosen oil effect product.

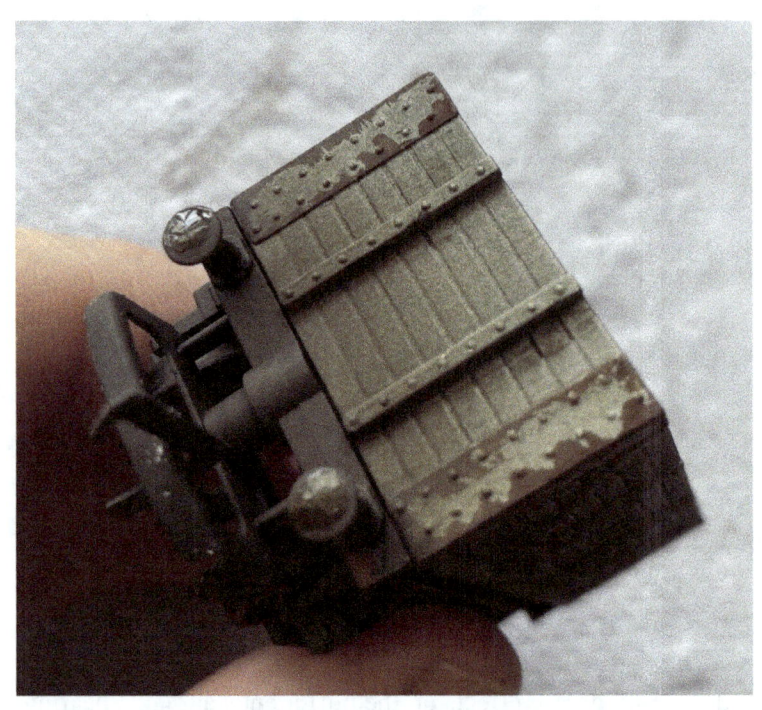

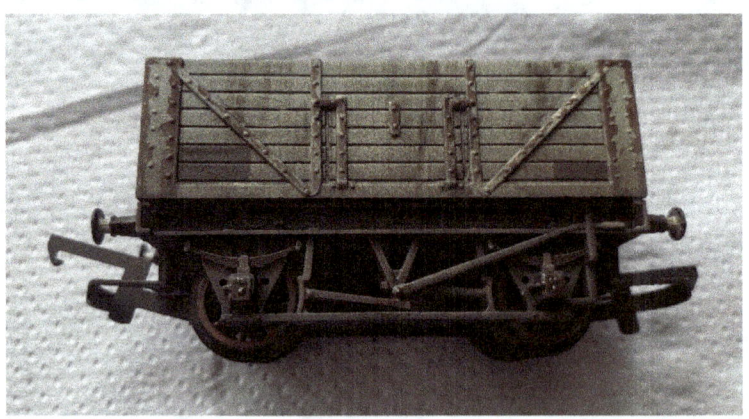

Leave the oil effects to dry fully.

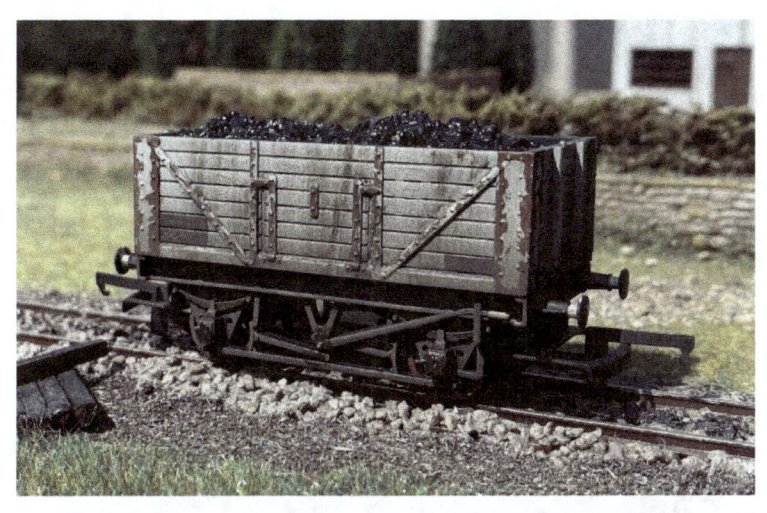

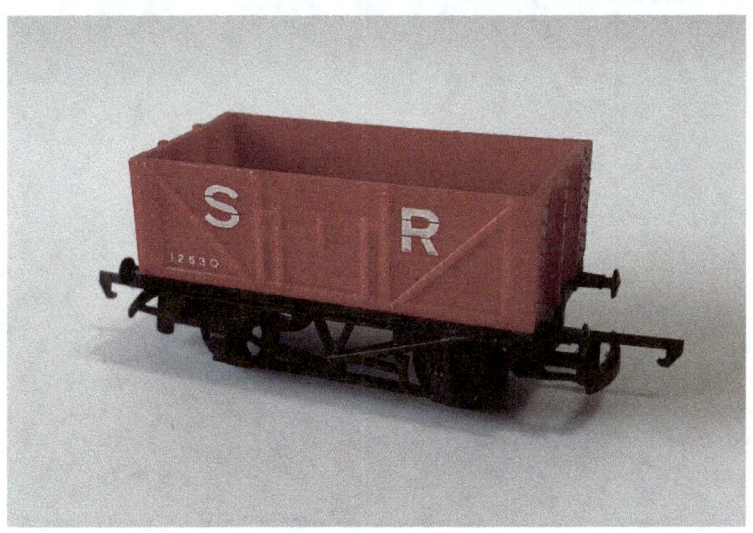

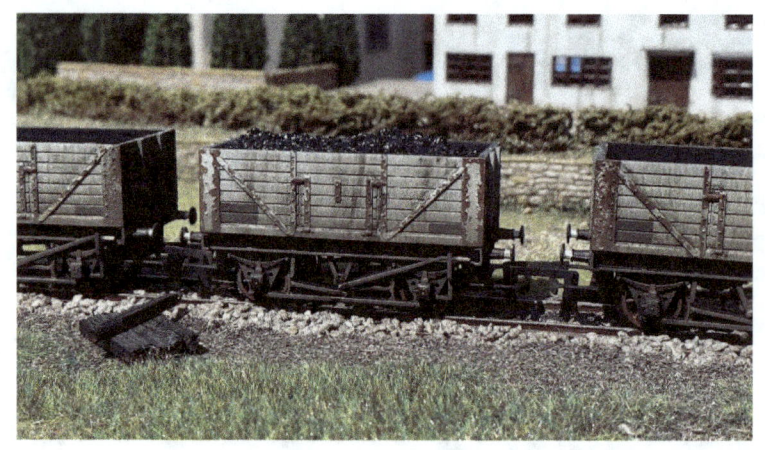

# Chapter 9 – Hornby Prime Pork Van
(pre-shade, repaint, weathering, dot filter on roof)

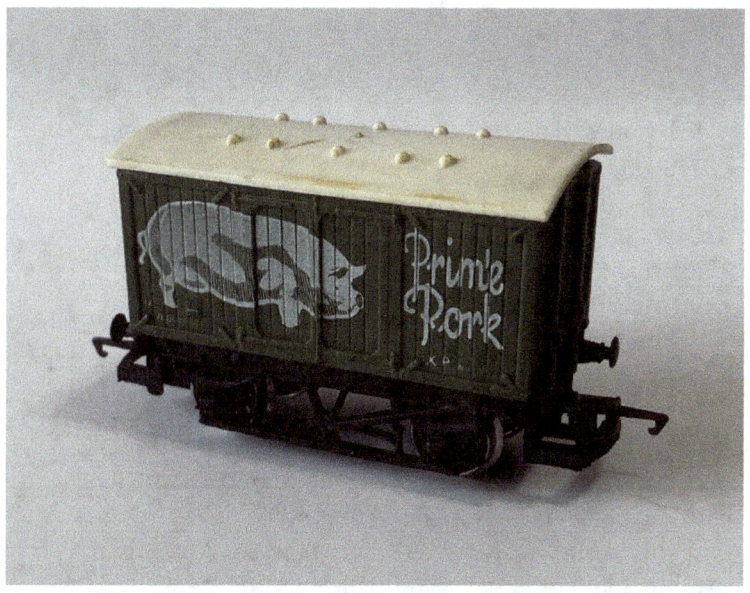

This project will turn a Hornby Prime Pork van into a more realistic BR ventilated van using a pre-shading technique to provide colour modulation in the final repainting.

Used ventilated vans and similar types in gawdy, unrealistic liveries are readily available from Hornby, Triang and Lima. This exact set of techniques can also be used very effectively to improve the appearance of Triang and Hornby cattle wagons.

As usual, before starting the painting process, the wagon will get a scrub in water and washing up liquid, followed by a thorough rinse and left to air dry for a day. However, in this case, the body must be carefully prised from the chassis prior to painting to be dealt with separately. You may find it more convenient to separate the body and chassis prior to cleaning (see Step 1).

In addition to the equipment listed in Chapter 2, for this project you will require the following items or suitable equivalents.

| Item | What I used |
|---|---|
| Oil Brusher | Mig Ammo, Medium Grey |
| Oil Brusher | Mig Ammo, Dark Brown |
| Oil Brusher | Mig Ammo, Star ship Filth |
| Grey acrylic primer | Halfords aerosol, grey primer |
| Black acrylic primer | Halfords aerosol, matt black |
| Acrylic paint | Mig Ammo, Rubber & Tyres |
| Acrylic paint | Mig Ammo, Old Rust |
| Acrylic paint | Mig Ammo, White |
| Acrylic paint | Mig Ammo, Matt Aluminium |
| Acrylic paint | Mig Ammo, Matt Black |
| Acrylic paint | Vallejo Model Air, Mud Brown |
| Acrylic paint | Rail Match, Frame Dirt |
| Acrylic varnish, satin | Mig Ammo Lucky Varnish |
| Acrylic varnish, matt | Winsor & Newton Galleria |
| Enamel wash | Mig Ammo, Star ship Wash |
| Oil effect | Mig Ammo, Fresh Engine Oil |
| Size 4 brush | |
| Size 5/0 brush | |
| Size 10/0 brush | |
| Size 2/0 brush | |

| Size 10 brush | |
| --- | --- |

## Step 1

As this project will involve repainting of the wagon body, it is easiest to conduct this after removing the wagon from the chassis. Triang and Hornby wagon bodies secured by means of the four melted posts in the floor corners can be carefully levered away from the chassis using a small screwdriver.

Once removed, if the post ends are burred over, they can be trimmed off using a sprue cutter. Likewise, floor holes can be cleared out using a small drill bit to aid reassembly.

Remove the wagon roof if possible (some Triang versions have a glued roof).

## Step 2

Once separated from each other, the wagon body and roof are sprayed with a grey acrylic primer using the airbrush or an aerosol can.

It is also worthwhile giving the chassis a coat of black primer or matt black while it is separated.

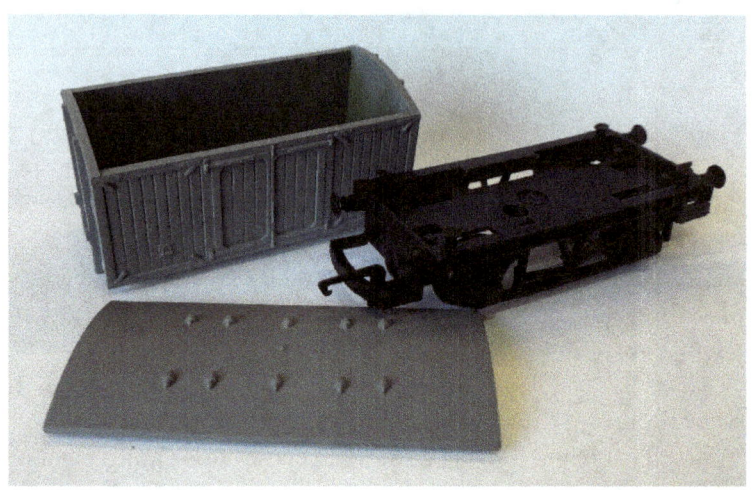

**Step 3**

Once the primer is dry, details on the wagon body exterior and roof are carefully highlighted using matt black acrylic paint in the airbrush.

This will provide a degree of colour modulation once the wagon is repainted.

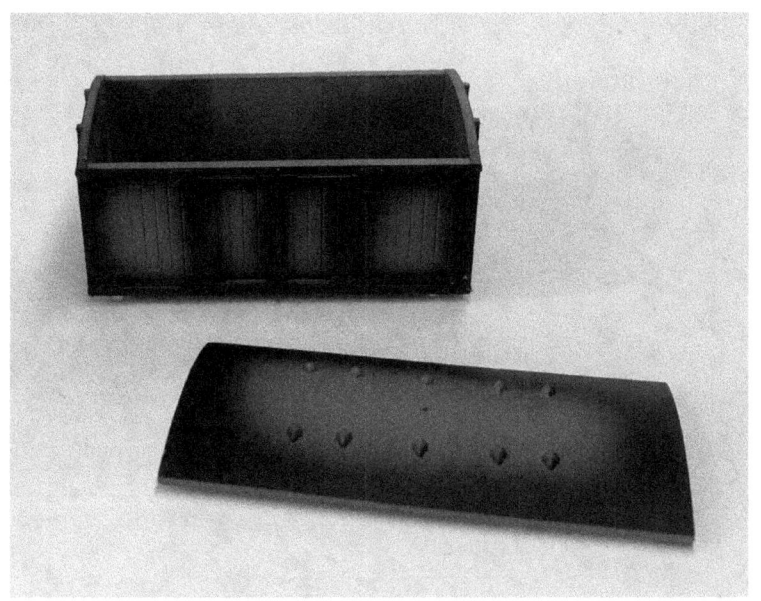

**Step 4**

Once the pre-shading paint is dry, the wagon body is repainted with light airbrush coats of Mud Brown, ensuring that the contrast between underlying black and grey areas is still visible.

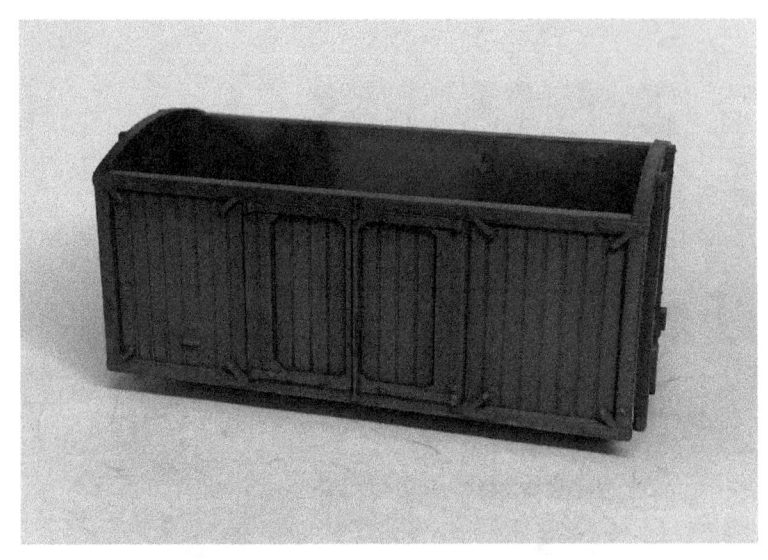

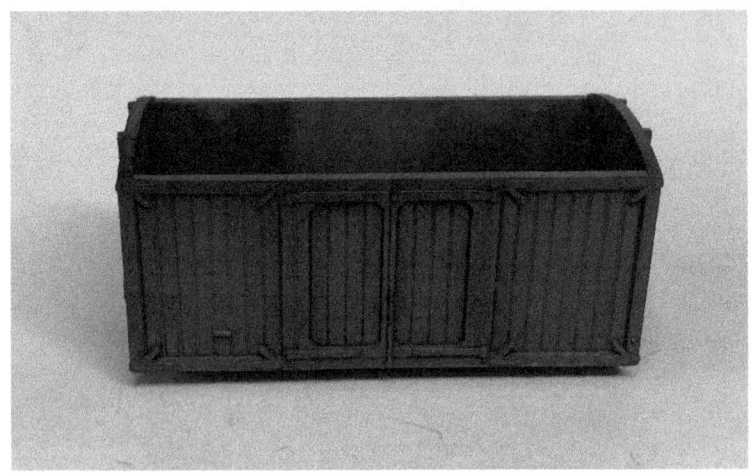

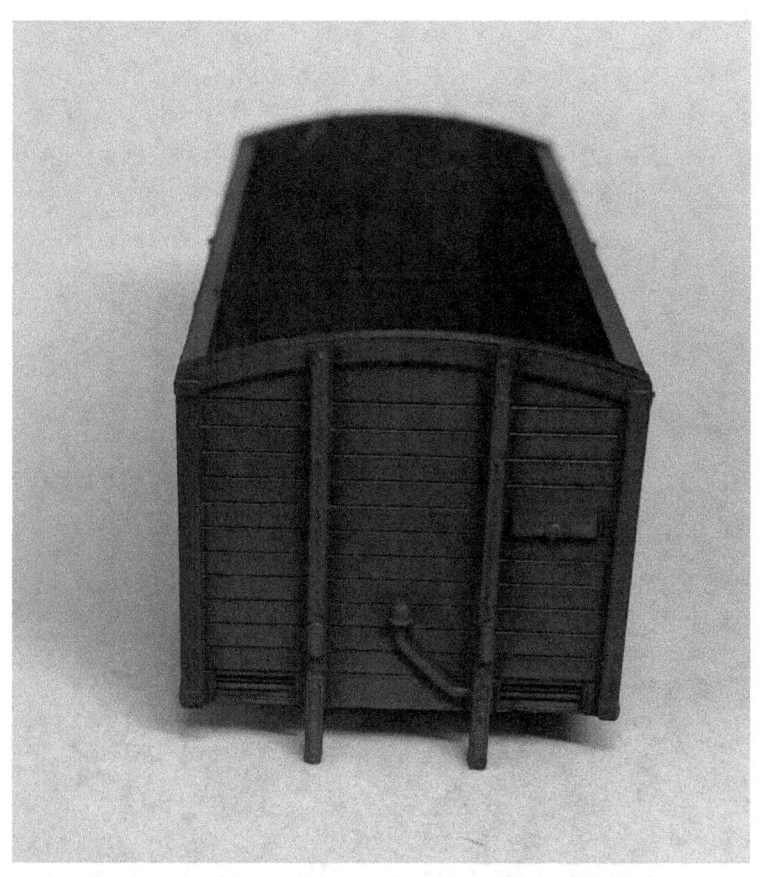

Likewise, the roof is repainted with light airbrush coats of Rubber & Tyres ensuring that the contrast between underlying black and grey areas is still visible.

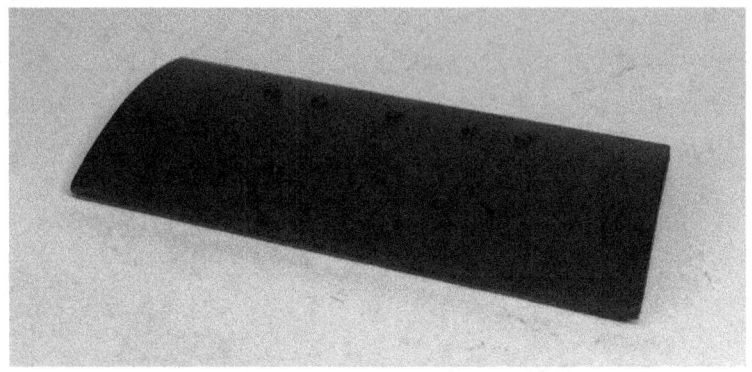

## Step 5

This is followed by hand painting rusty paint chips onto the chassis and ironwork using a 5/0 or 10/0 brush.

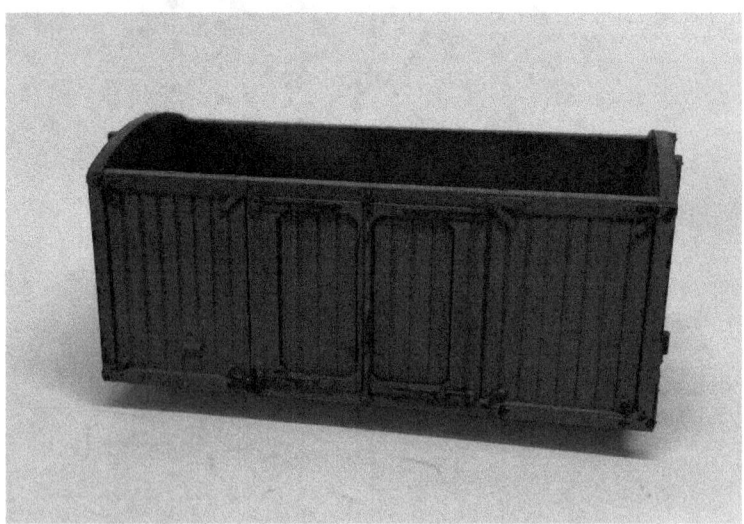

## Step 6

The wheels are painted in rust colour using a 2/0 brush.
Picking out cast iron brake shoes and leaf springs with the rust
colour.

## Step 7

The final painting stage involves picking out the buffer shafts
in our silver acrylic colour and the brake lever handles using
white acrylic using a 5/0 or 10/0 brush.

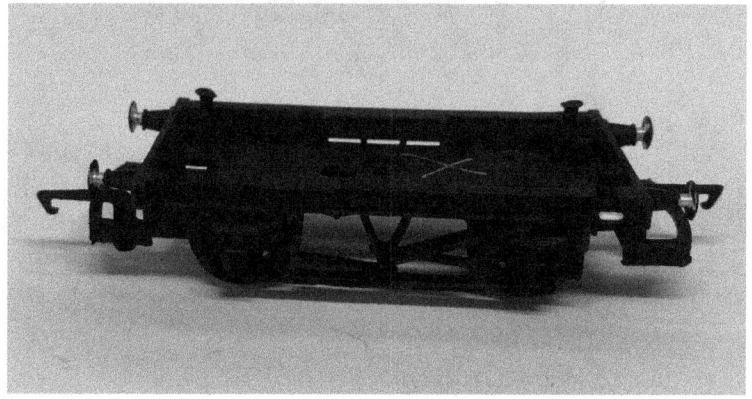

## Step 8

Once dry, the wagon can now be reassembled.

A dab of rubberised superglue around each post will secure
the body in position after test fitting prior to glue application.

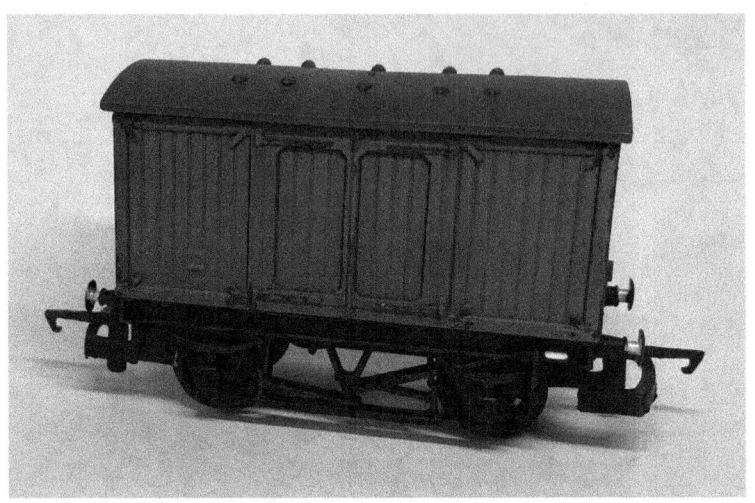

**Step 9**

Once the acrylic paint is fully dry, apply a coat of satin acrylic varnish using the airbrush.

Allow the varnish to fully cure for 24 hours.

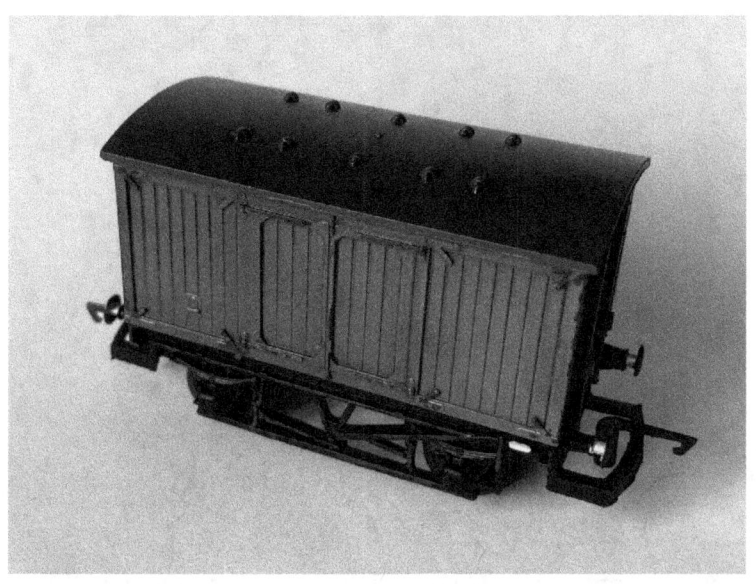

**Step 10**

Apply a few small dots of the dark brown oil paint along the upslope lines of the rain deflectors and around the roof vents. Next, apply a few random dots around the roof of the dark grey and medium grey oil paints.

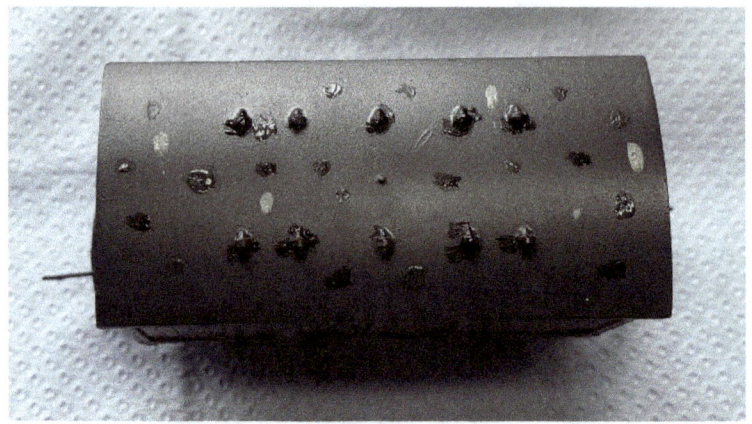

Moisten a Size 10 brush in enamel thinners and dry on a paper towel until no thinners is transferred to the towel.

Using the brush, spread the dark brown oil paint around the roof protrusions and then wipe the brush on the paper towel.

Starting from the centre line of the roof, use single brush strokes to drag streaks of the oil paints to the edge of the roof. Periodically wipe the brush on the paper towel. Repeat for the other side of the roof.

Repeat the single stroke streaking for both sides of the roof and wipe the brush on the paper towel.

Finally, with a rapid two directional brush stroke action pass over the entire roof blurring the oil paint streaks.

Leave to dry for 24 hours.

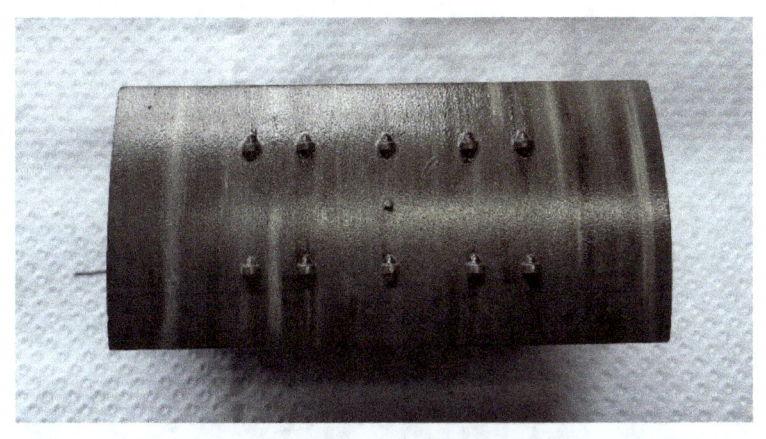

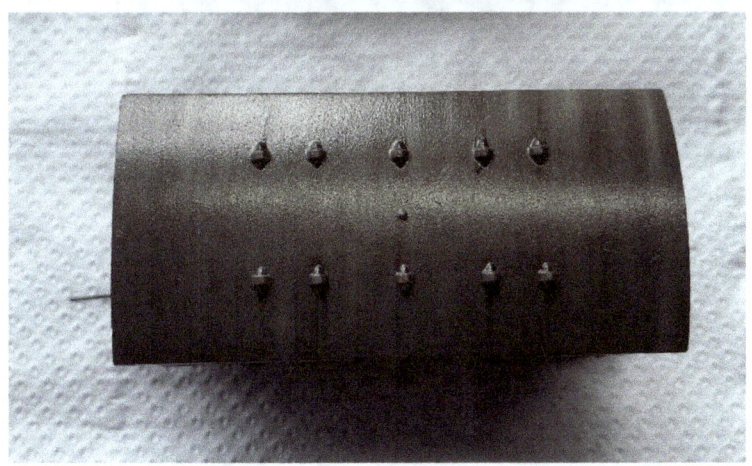

137

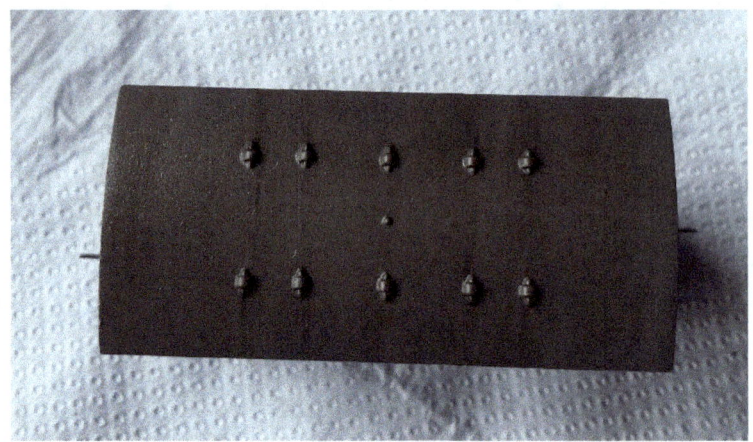

## Step 11

Using a 2/0 brush, apply the well shaken enamel Star ship Wash to each raised or recessed detail on the wagon body and allow the wash to flow along the moulded edges.

Leave the wash to dry for around 30 minutes.

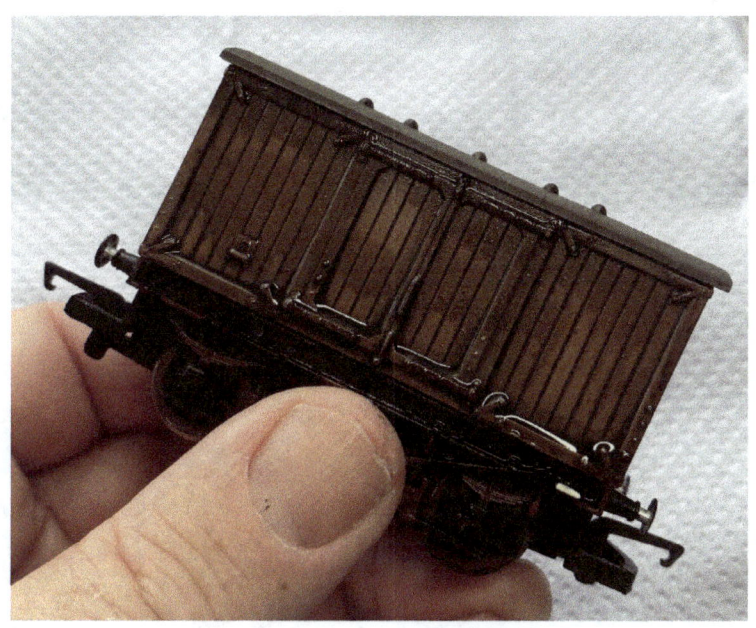

**Step 12**

Once the wash has dried sufficiently, remove the excess wash using a broad tipped size 10 brush moistened in odourless enamel thinners.

Leave to dry for 24 hours.

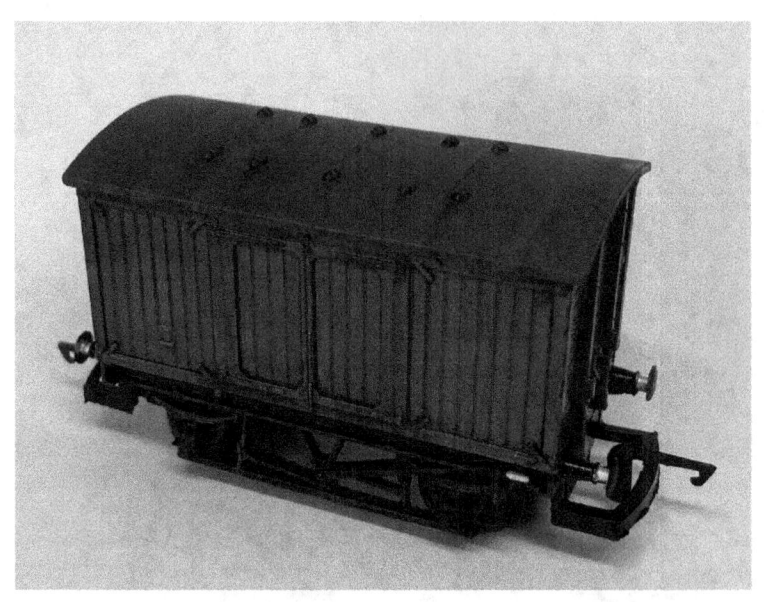

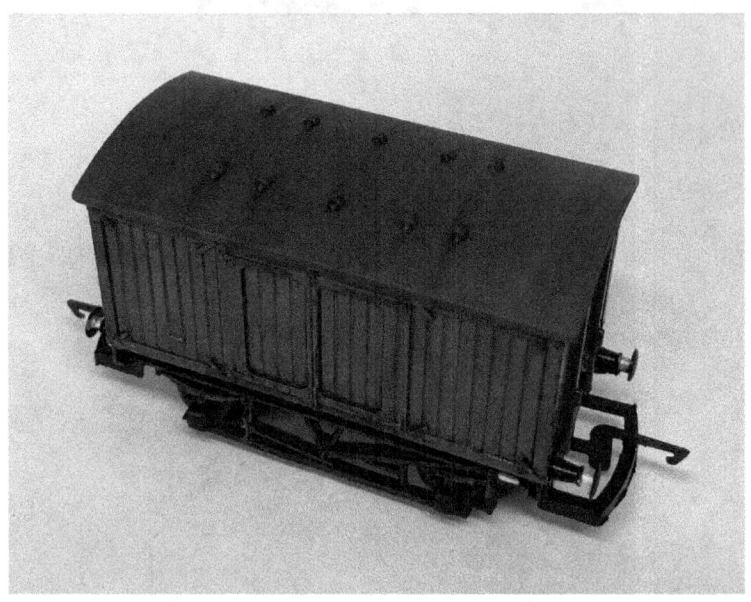

**Step 13**

Use the airbrush to apply a misted coat of our chosen dirt colour to the chassis and lower regions of the wagon body and body ends.

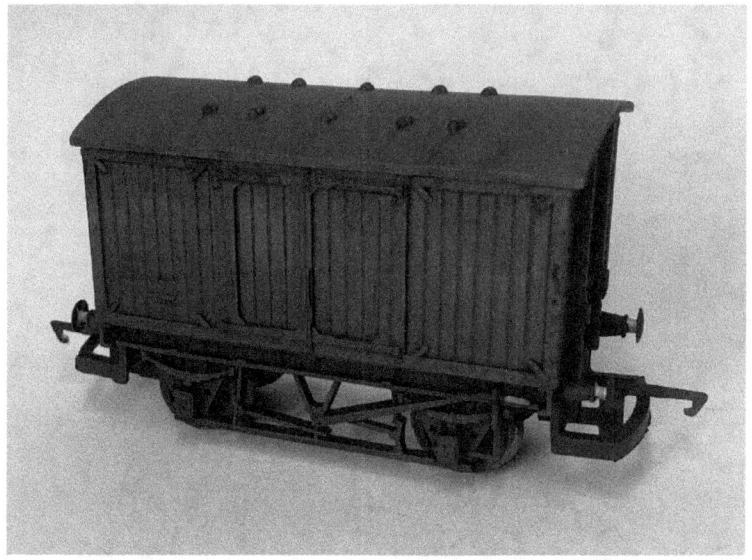

**Step 14**

Apply two coats of matt acrylic varnish using the airbrush.

**Step 15**

Add oil and grease effects on the buffer ends and axle bearing boxes, applied using a 5/0 brush and our chosen oil effect product.

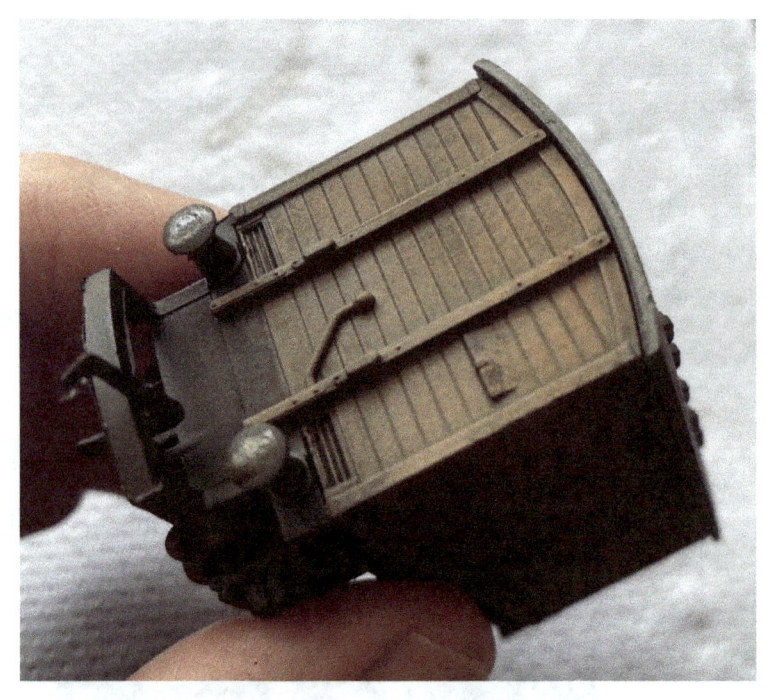

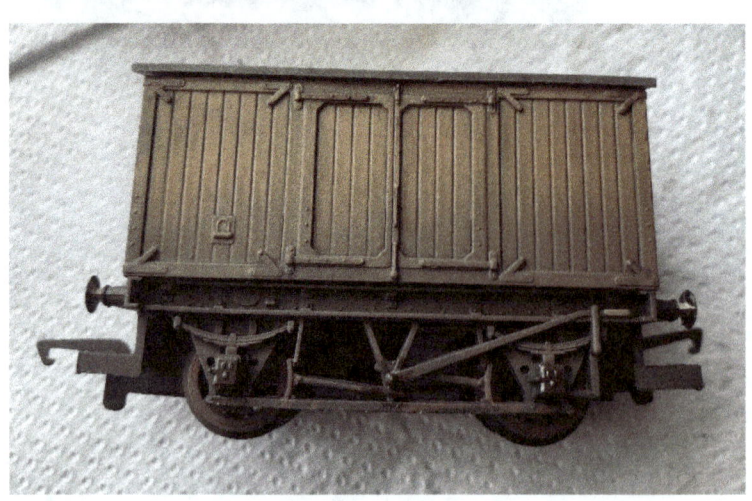

142

Leave the oil effects to dry fully.

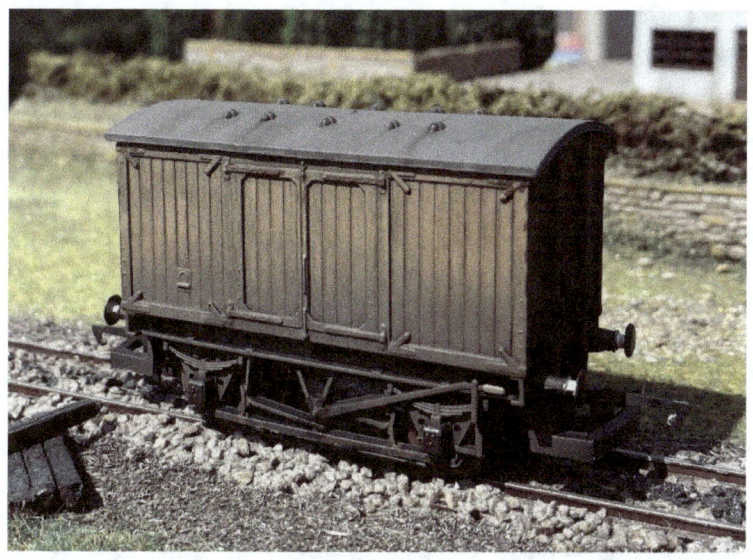

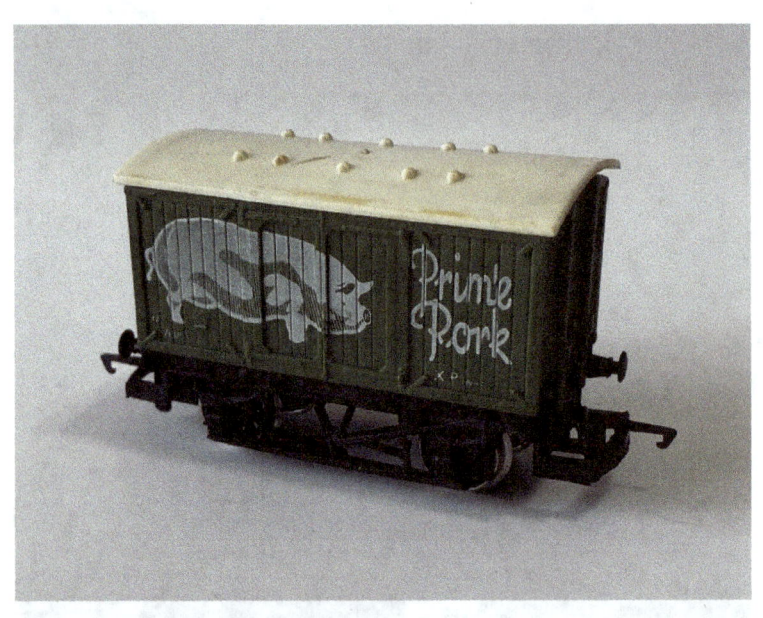

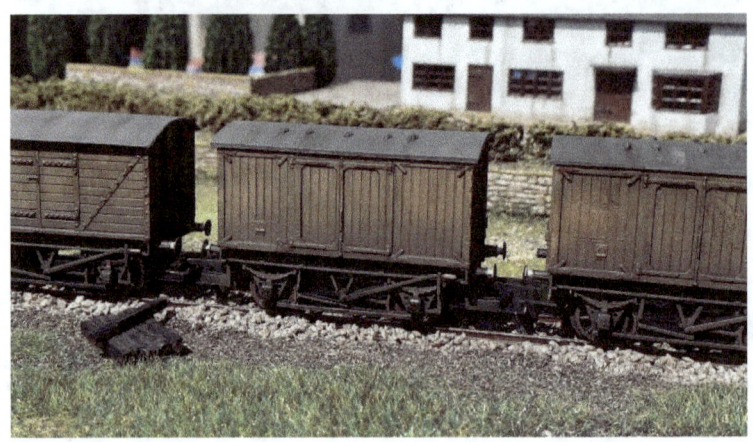

# Chapter 10 – Hornby 12t Tank Wagon
## (repaint, hairspray chipping)

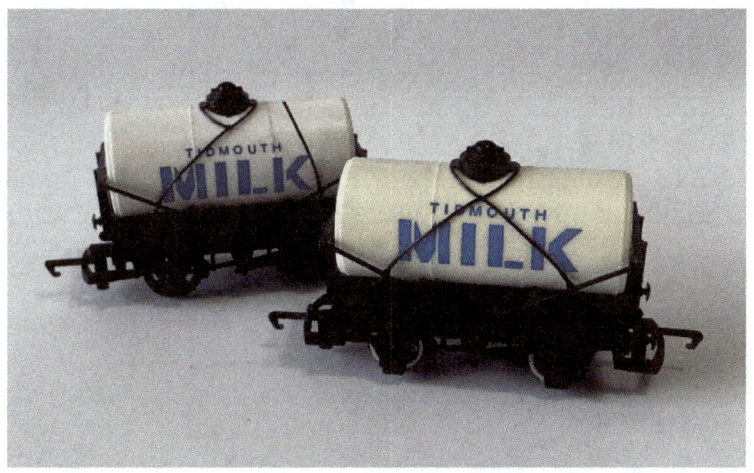

This project will transform the appearance of a classic toy-like Hornby or Triang tanker wagon using the earlier techniques with the addition of the use of a hairspray chipping technique.

As with the previous projects, the model will require some dismantling and washing prior to painting commencing.

In addition to the equipment listed in Chapter 2, for this project you will require the following items or suitable equivalents:

| Item | What I used |
| --- | --- |
| Grey acrylic primer | Halfords aerosol, grey primer |
| Black acrylic primer | Halfords aerosol, matt black |
| Acrylic paint | Mig Ammo, British Olive Drab |
| Acrylic paint | Mig Ammo, Old Rust |
| Acrylic paint | Mig Ammo, Medium Rust |
| Acrylic paint | Mig Ammo, Dark Rust |
| Acrylic paint | Vallejo Model Air, Burnt Umber |
| Acrylic paint | Mig Ammo, Matt Aluminium |
| Acrylic paint | Rail Match, Frame Dirt |
| Acrylic varnish, satin | Mig Ammo Lucky Varnish |
| Acrylic varnish, matt | Winsor & Newton Galleria |
| Oil effect | Mig Ammo, Fresh Engine Oil |
| Diesel effect | Mig Ammo, Fuel Stains |
| Size 5/0 brush | |
| Size 10/0 brush | |
| Size 2/0 brush | |
| Size 12 brush | |

Although not entirely necessary here, a simple stand like the one I used in this example is worth making from styrene modelling sheet.

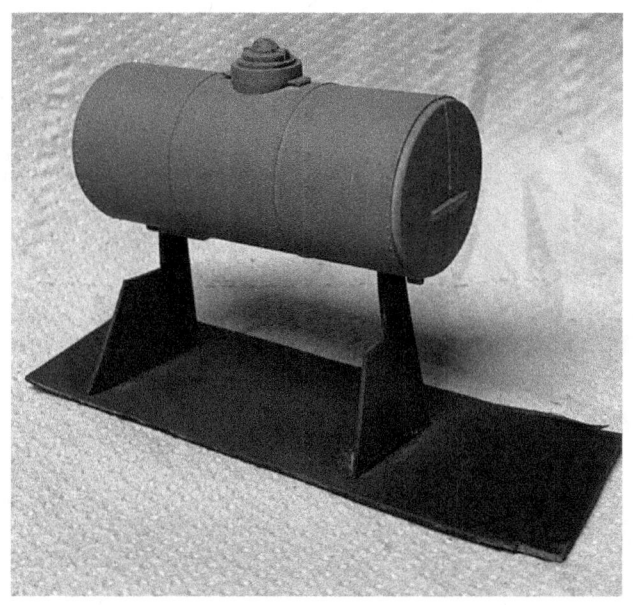

**Step 1**

Remove the tanker body from the chassis.

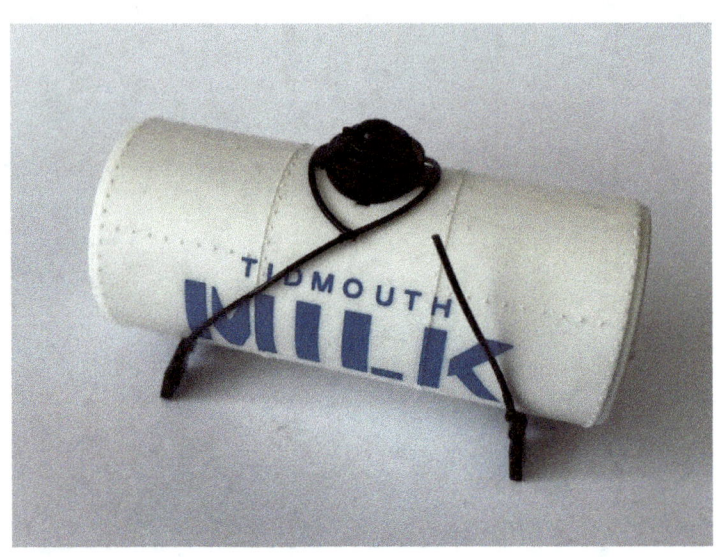

## Step 2

Remove damaged cross bracing, if present.

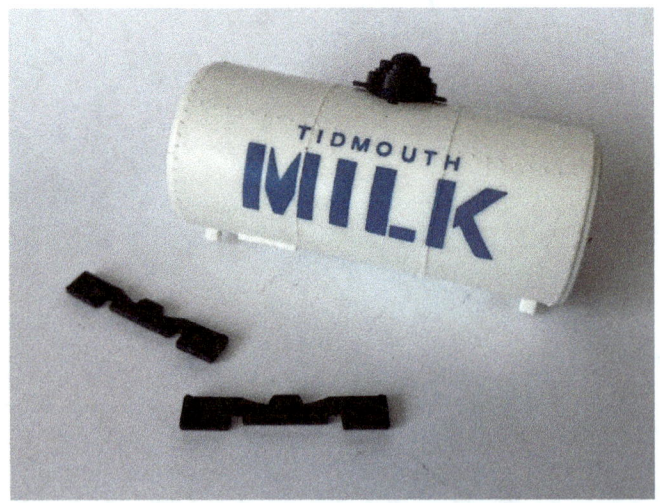

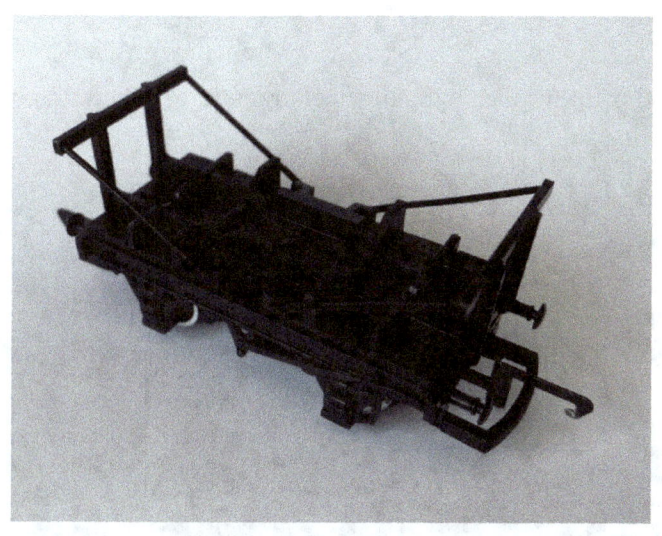

**Step 3**

Spray tanker body with grey acrylic primer and chassis assembly with black acrylic primer or matt black spray paint.

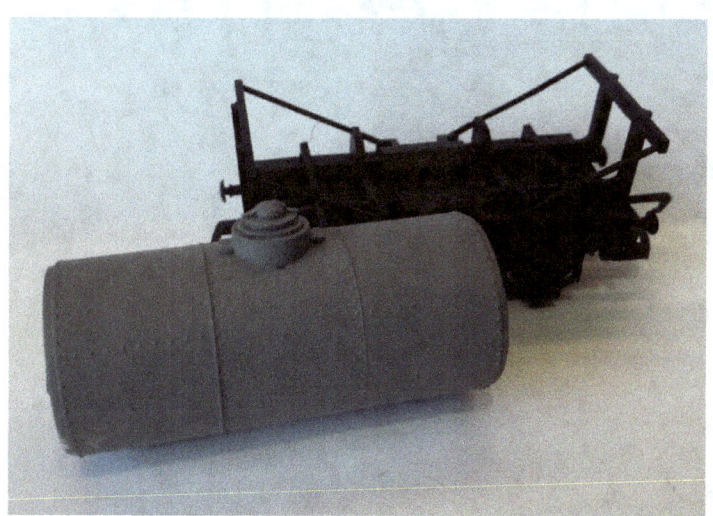

149

## Step 4

Hand paint wooden parts of superstructure with burnt umber acrylic paint.

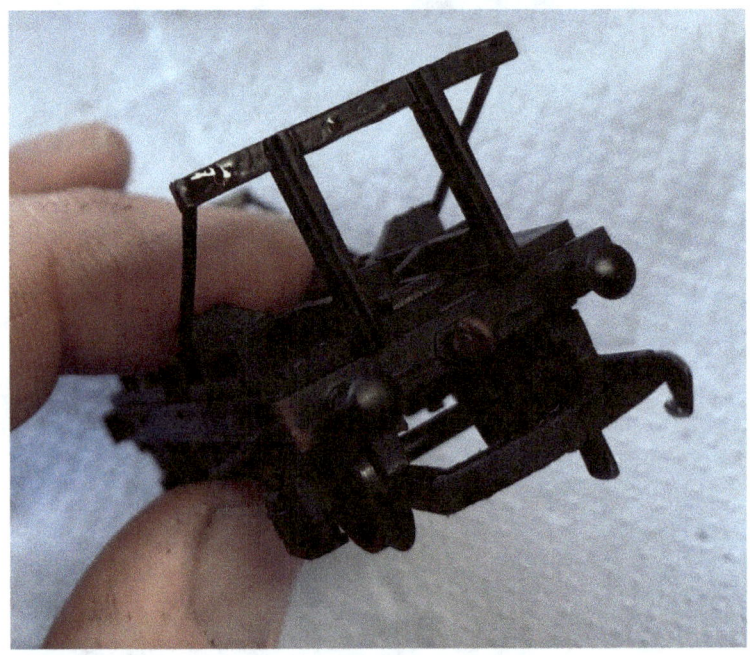

## Step 5

Hand paint rusty paint chips onto chassis assembly, picking out brake blocks and springs. Hand paint wheels rust coloured acrylic.

Pick out buffer shafts in silver acrylic and brake handles in white acrylic.

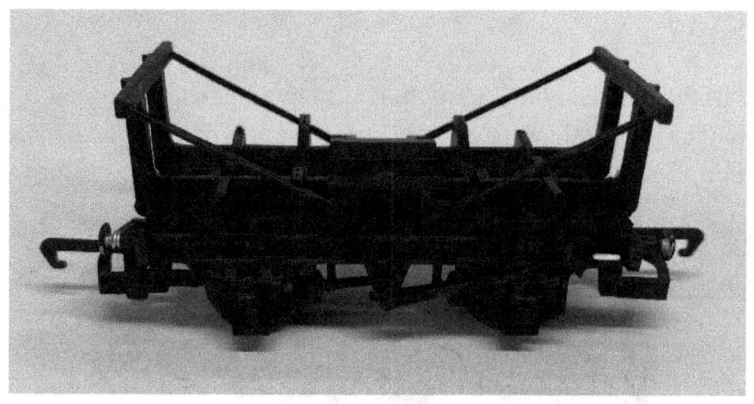

## Step 6

Airbrush paint the tanker body in our base rust colour (Ammo Old Rust) and allow to dry.

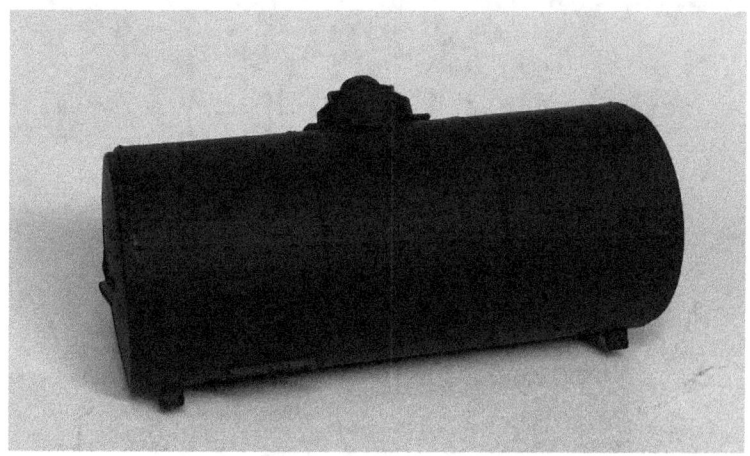

**Step 7**

Using a small sponge section held in tweezers, apply mottled patches of Medium Rust and Dark Rust acrylic over the tanker body and allow to dry for 24 hours.

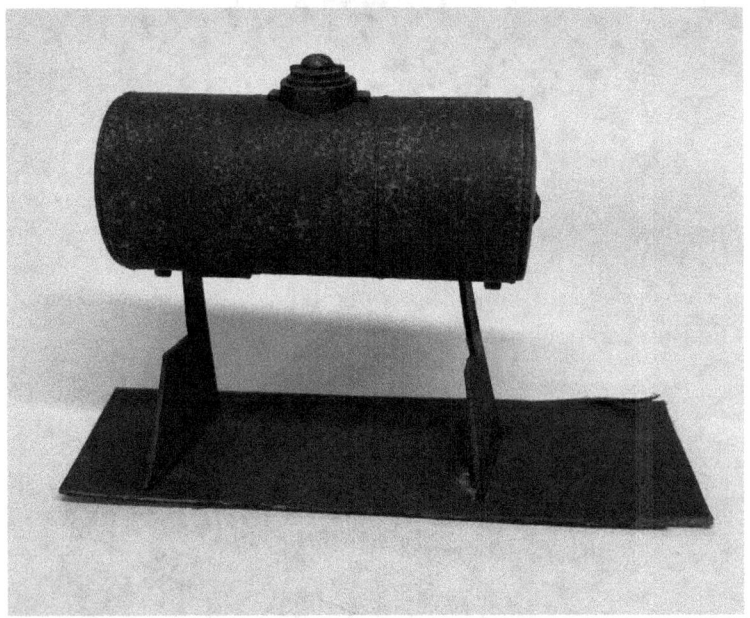

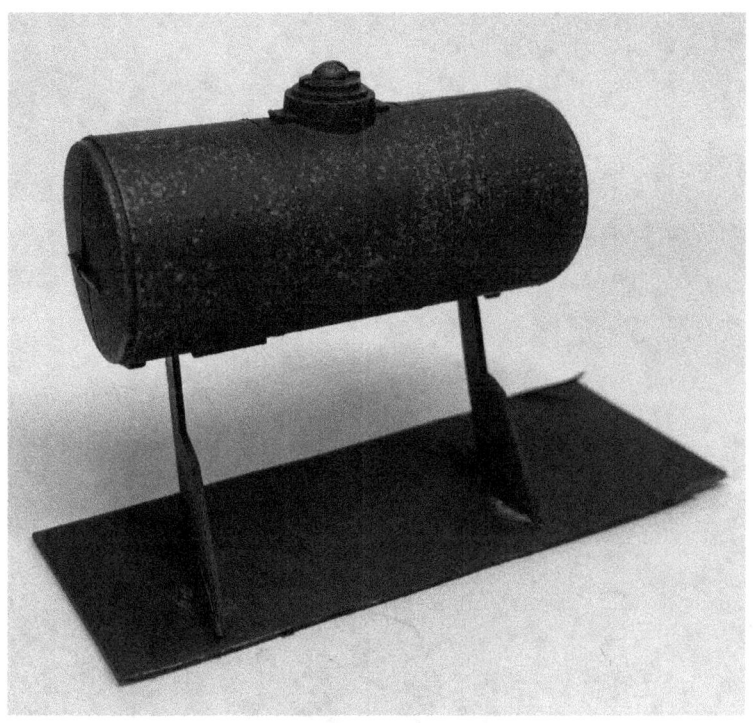

**Step 8**

Using an un-fragranced hairspray aerosol, lightly coat the tanker body with hairspray. Short bursts from around 200mm away work well.

I tend to conduct this outdoors as the hairspray smell is fairly strong and the mist settles out as a sticky mess.

Allow to dry for at least 30 minutes.

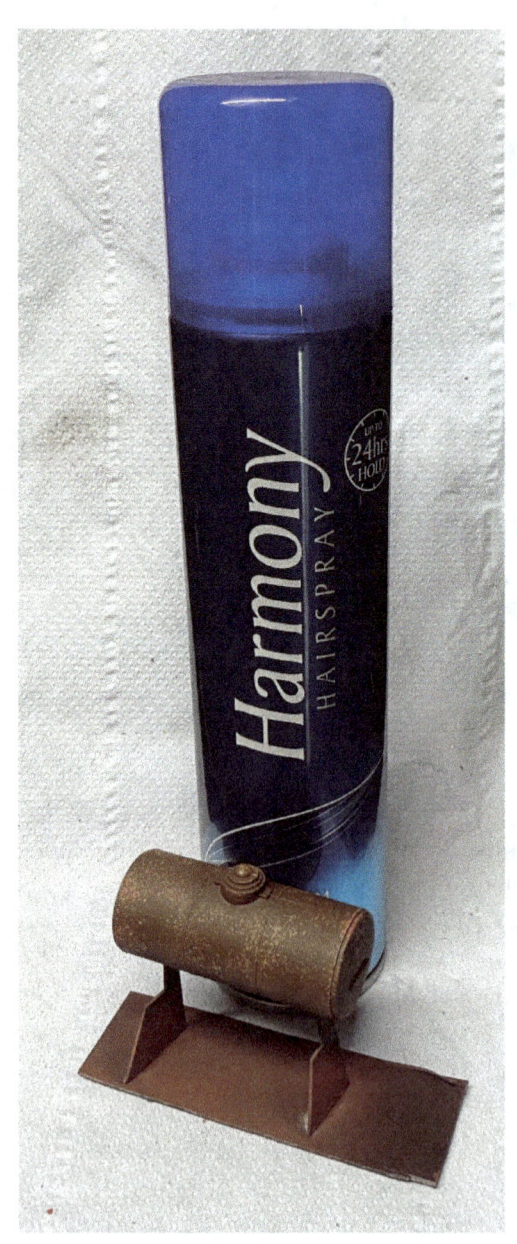

154

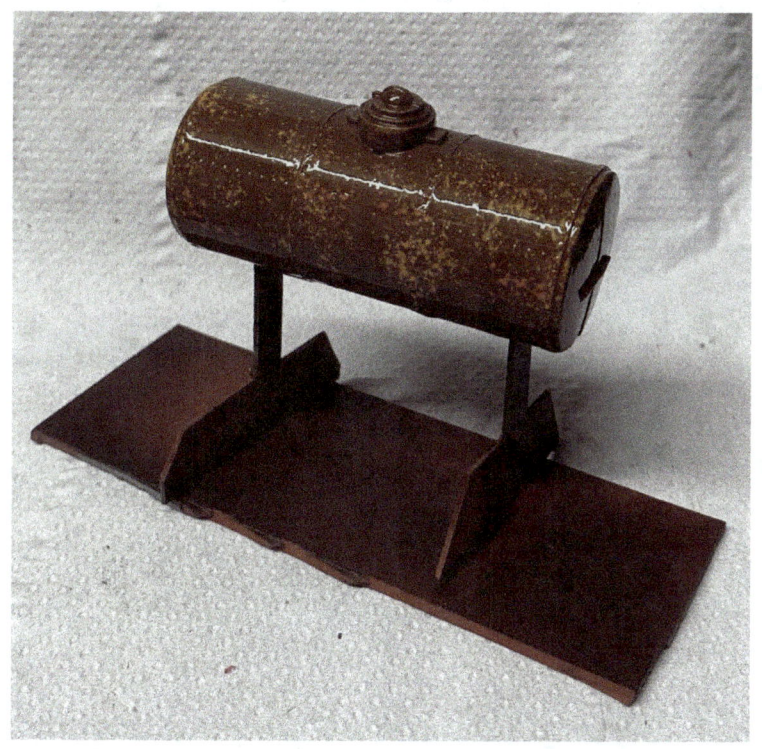

**Step 9**

Once the hairspray is fully dry, airbrush paint the tanker body with the desired colour (I have used Olive Drab in this example) with light coats and allow to dry for around 1 hour.

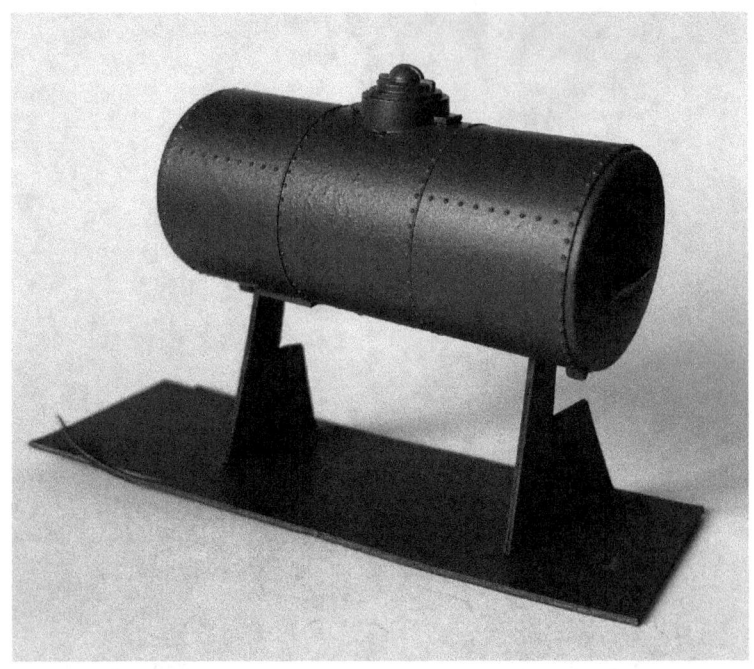

**Step 10**

Once acrylic paint has become completely touch dry, lightly coat the surface with cold water using a wide brush and allow the water to soak in for a few seconds.

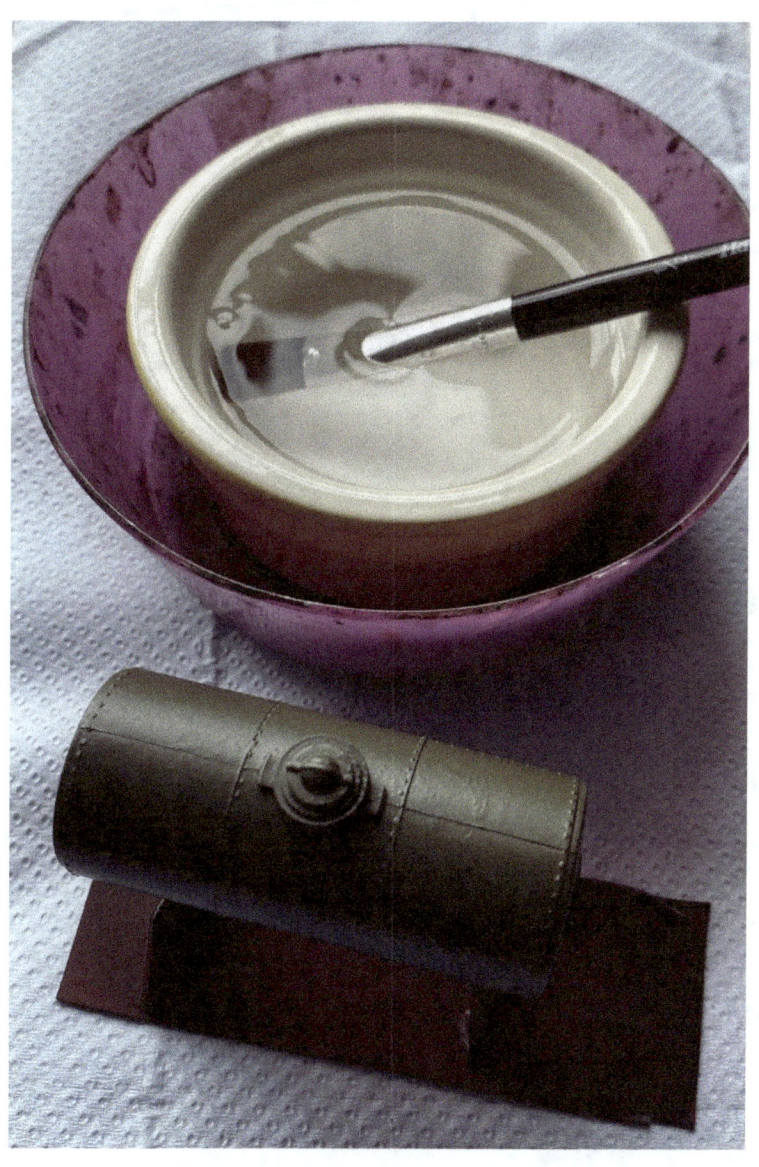

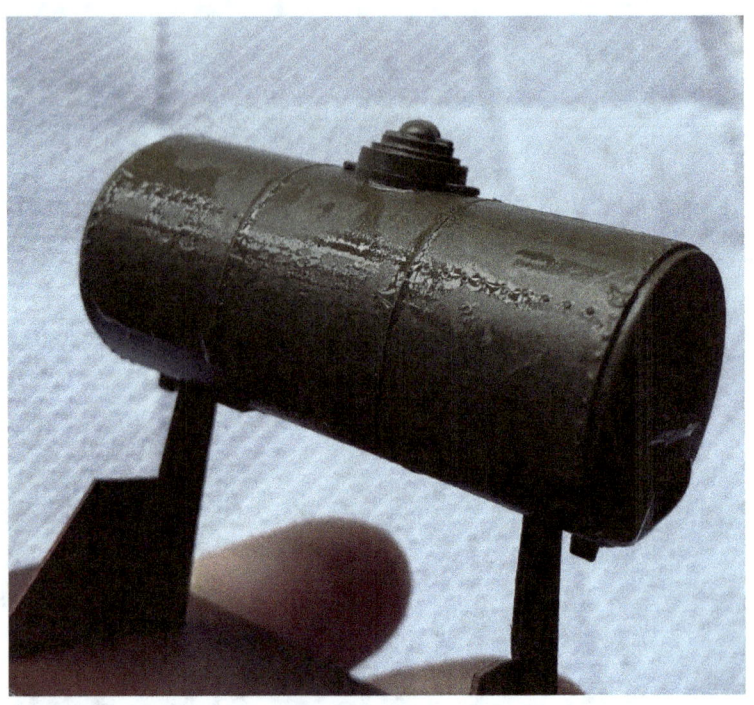

**Step 12**

Using a short-bristled brush moistened with cold water, start to gently work at the paint surface in areas where you want chipping to appear such as plate edges.

Continue until the desired extent of chipping is obtained.

Once complete, carefully dab the surface with a paper towel to remove excess water and any foam (DO NOT WIPE the surface as this will drag the paint off).

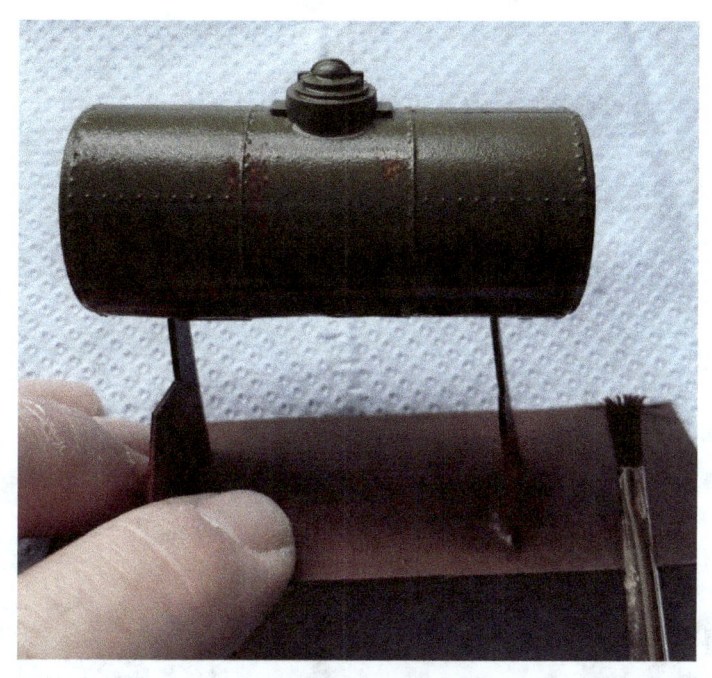

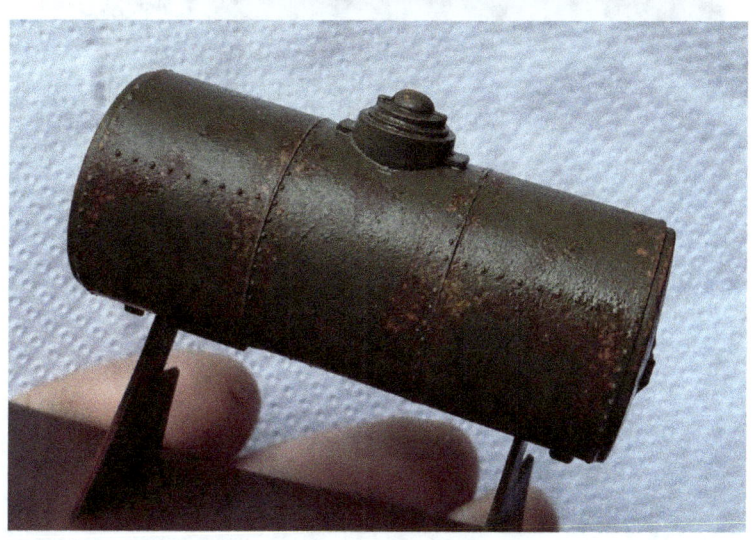

**Step 13**

Leave the tanker body to dry for 24 hours.

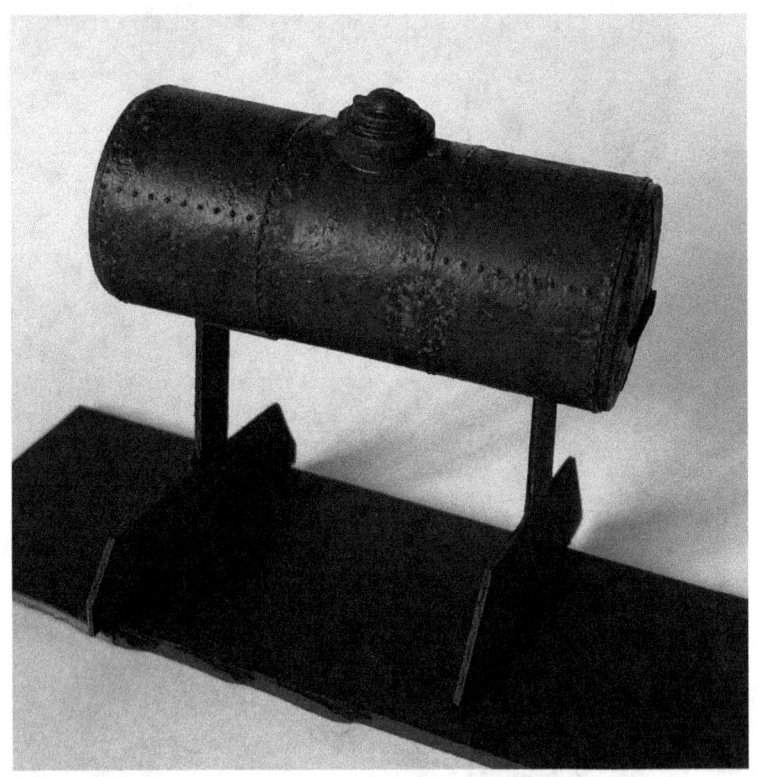

**Step 14**

Reassemble the tanker body onto the chassis, ensuring your hands are completely dry.

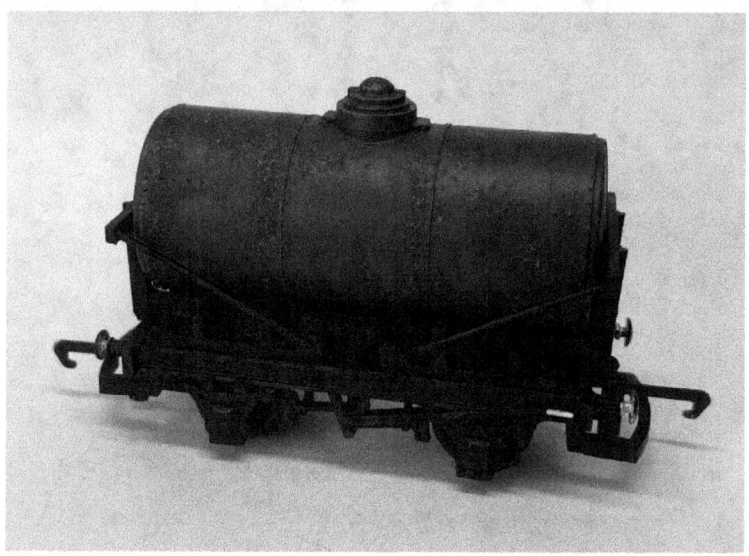

**Step 15**

Use the airbrush to apply a misted coat of our chosen dirt colour to the chassis and lower regions of the wagon body and body ends.

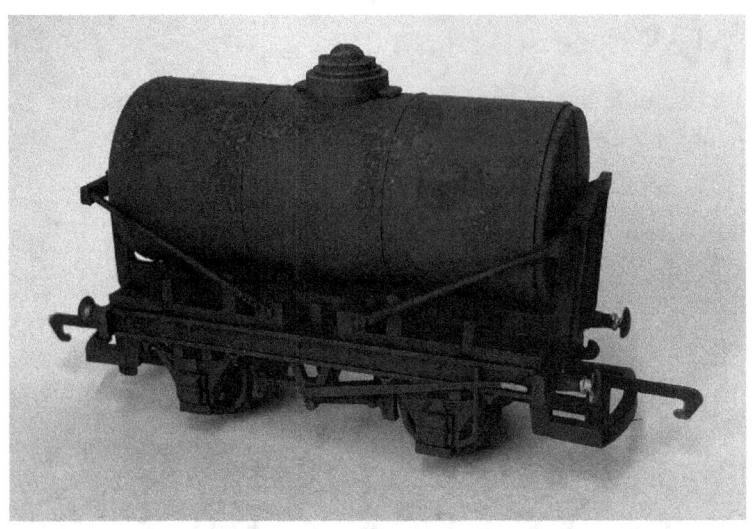

**Step 16**

Apply two coats of matt acrylic varnish using the airbrush.

**Step 17**

Add oil and grease effects on the buffer ends and axle bearing boxes, applied using a 5/0 brush and our chosen oil effect product.

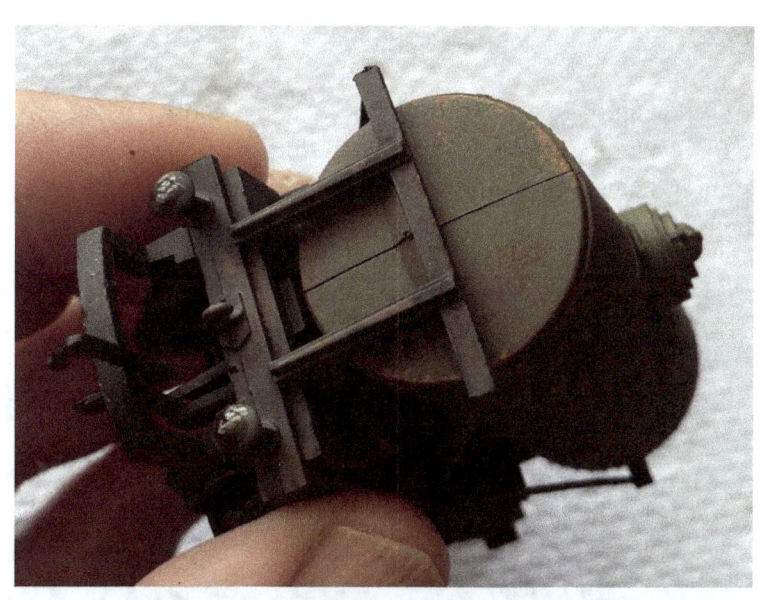

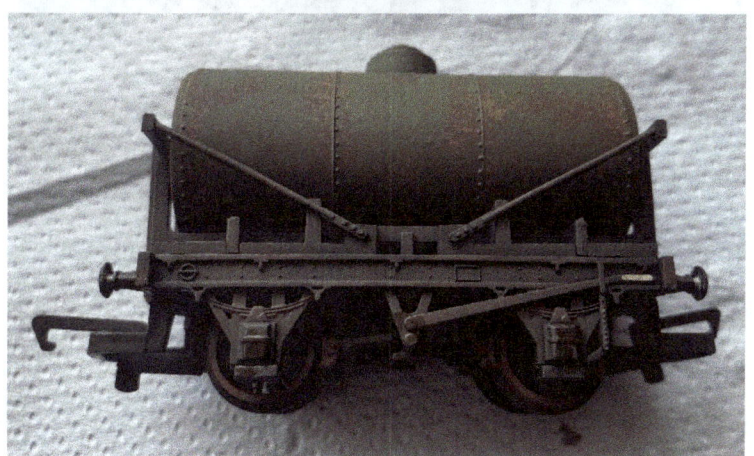

**Step 18**

Add fuel spillage effects to the tanker body, applied using a 5/0 brush and our chosen fuel stain effect product. The fuel stain product is best diluted with odourless enamel thinners before application in long streaks.

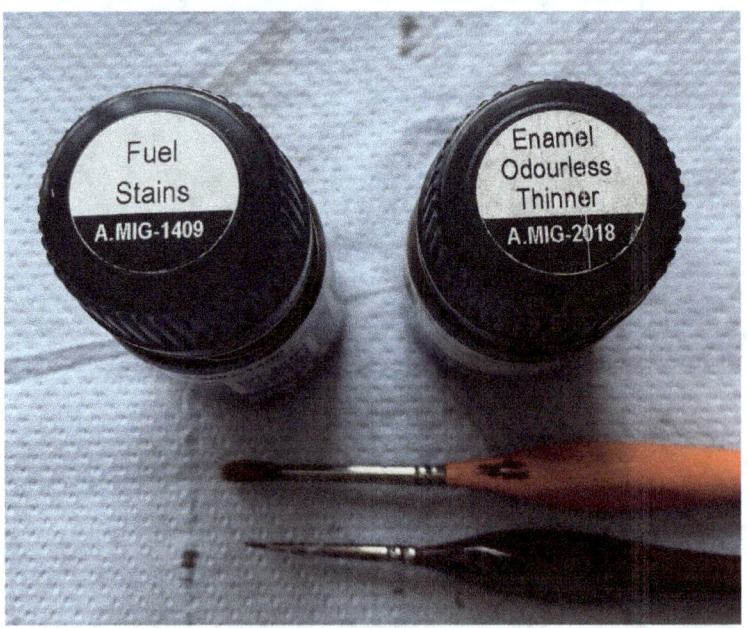

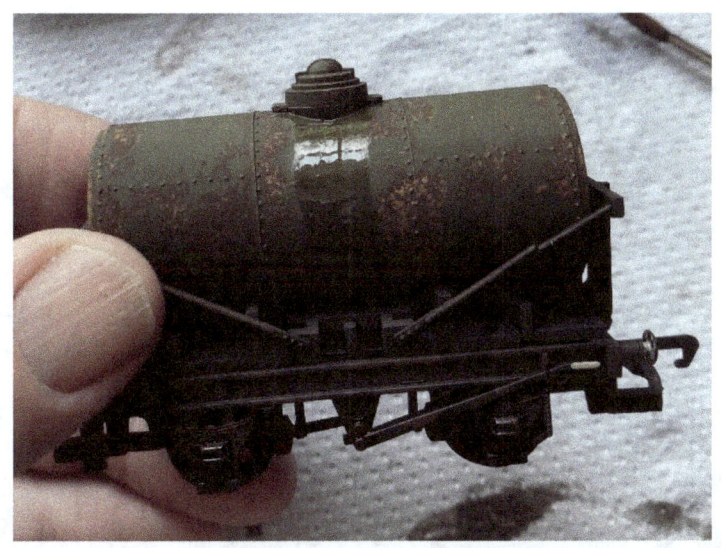

These streaks are then blended using downward strokes with a size 4 brush moistened in odourless enamel thinners.

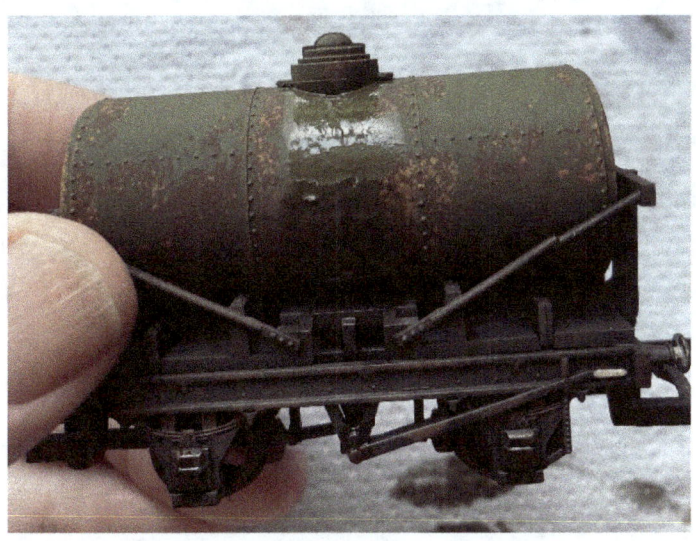

Leave the oil and fuel effects to dry fully.

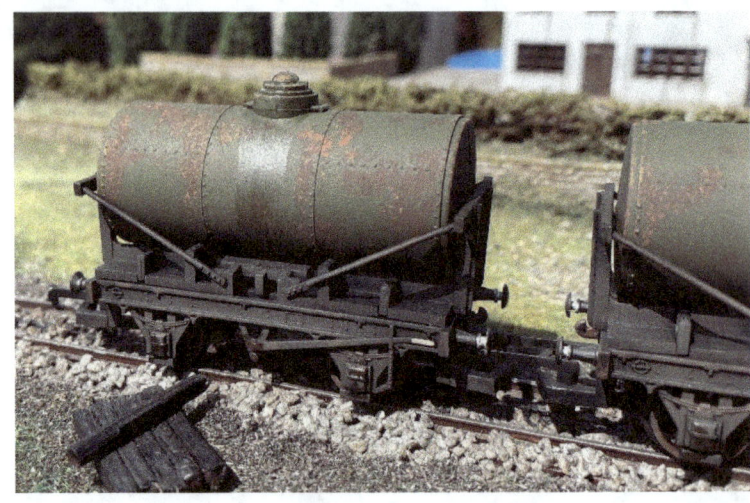

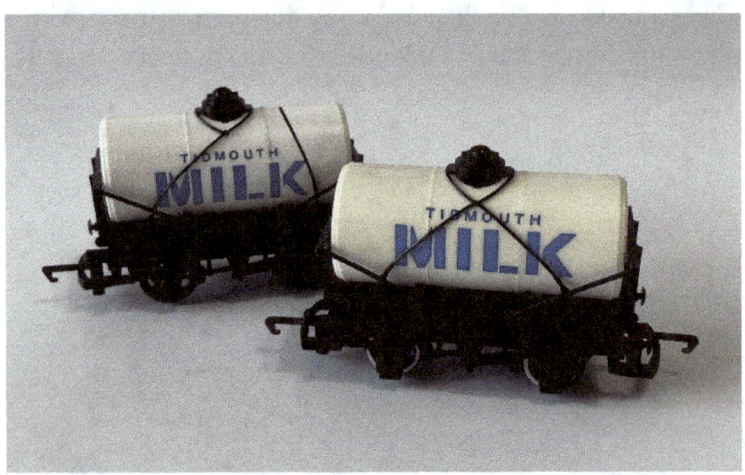

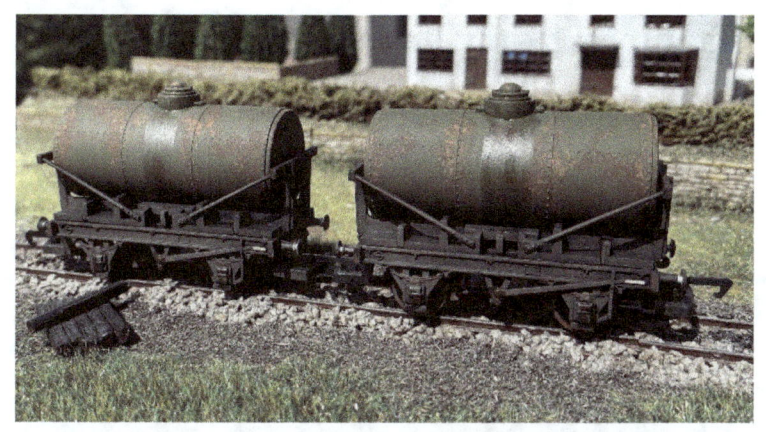

# Chapter 11 – Triang Cemflo Cement Tanker (repaint, weathering)

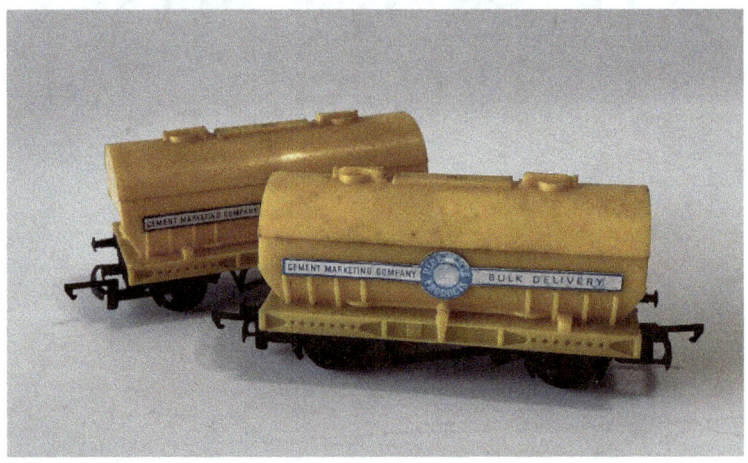

This project offers a drastic improvement in appearance thus far due to the use of colour modulation, not by pre-shading but by varying of colour shades in the yellow livery, to provide a more realistic effect than a single, flat colour tone.

As usual, before starting the painting process, the wagon will get a scrub in water and washing up liquid, followed by a thorough rinse and left to air dry for a day.

The bodies of these CEMFLO wagons can be difficult to remove without causing damage so I have opted to leave the wagon in one piece for painting.

Although I am not convinced that these wagons ever existed in a yellow livery, as depicted by Triang, I have stuck with that colour scheme to make the weathering a little more prominent than it would be on a grey or bare aluminium body.

In addition to the equipment listed in Chapter 2, for this project you will require the following items or suitable equivalents:

| Item | What I used |
|---|---|
| Grey acrylic primer | Halfords aerosol, grey primer |
| Acrylic paint | Mig Ammo, Old Rust |
| Acrylic paint | Mig Ammo, Gold Yellow |
| Acrylic paint | Mig Ammo, Yellow |
| Acrylic paint | Mig Ammo, Matt Black |
| Acrylic paint | Mig Ammo, Matt Aluminium |
| Acrylic paint | Rail Match, Frame Dirt |
| Acrylic varnish, satin | Mig Ammo Lucky Varnish |
| Acrylic varnish, matt | Winsor & Newton Galleria |
| Enamel wash | Mig Ammo, Nature Effects, Light Dust |
| Oil effect | Mig Ammo, Fresh Engine Oil |
| Masking agent | Humbrol Maskol |
| Size 1 brush | |
| Size 5/0 brush | |
| Size 10/0 brush | |
| Size 2/0 brush | |

## Step 1

As this project is based on wagons with fully intact paper labels, I have opted to retain them.

The first step is to protect the paper labels themselves from the masking agent by applying a coat of satin acrylic varnish over them.

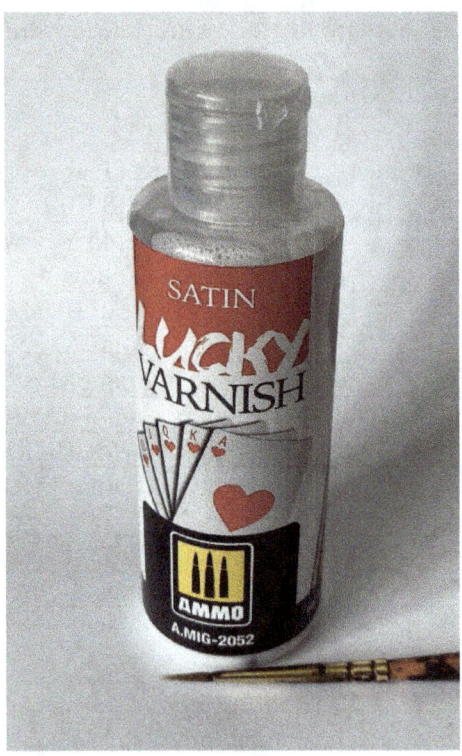

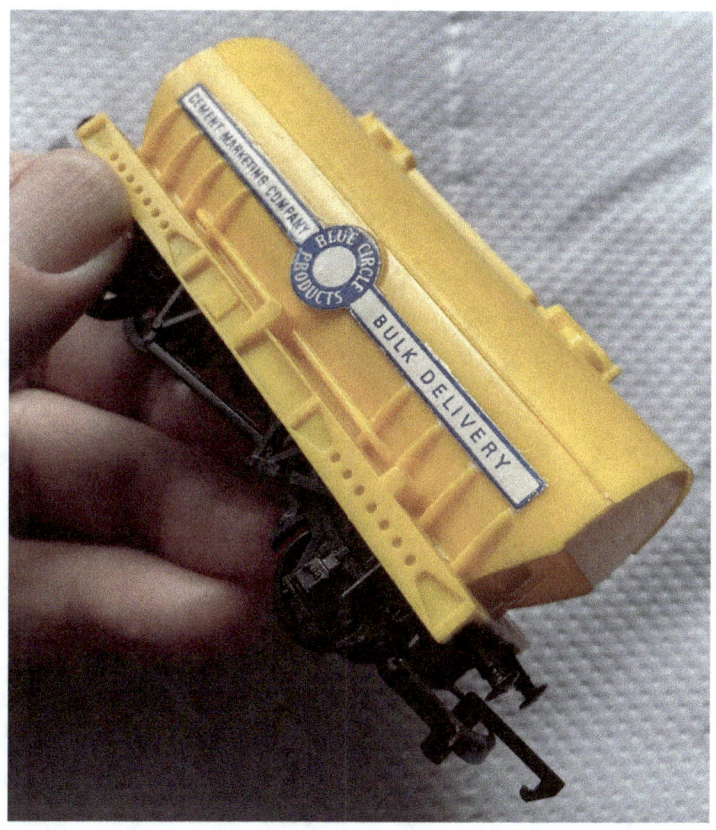

**Step 2**

Once the satin varnish is fully cured, we need to protect the labels for the painting phase.

To do this, I applied Humbrol Maskol agent which is a latex paste and rather tricky to spread as it dries so quickly. I tend to use a dabbing action with a short-bristled brush to build it up in a thick enough coat to aid later removal.

Try not to get Maskol beyond the label edges, if possible, this will reduce the amount of touching up required after removal.

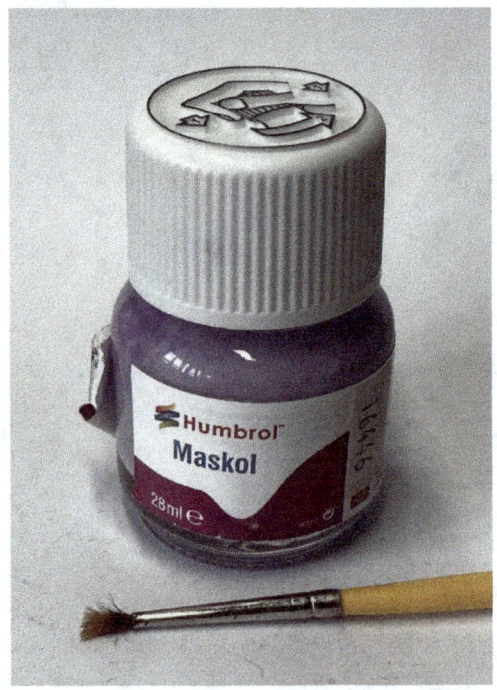

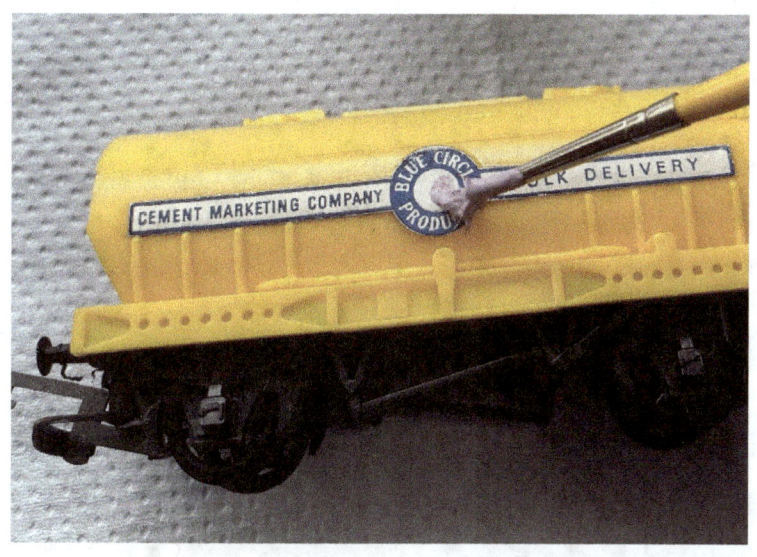

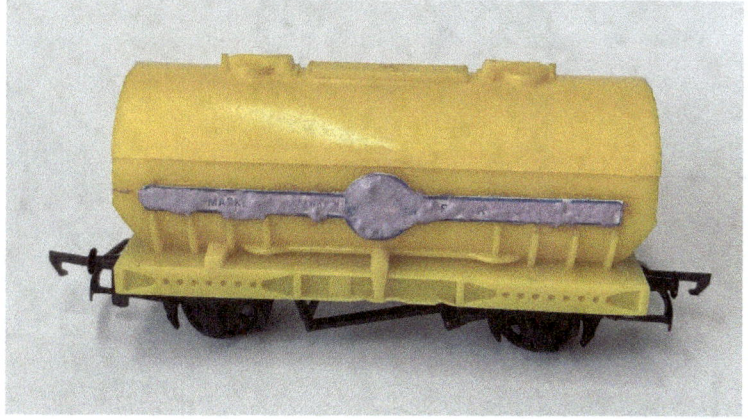

## Step 3

Once the Maskol is dry, it is time to address something that is an issue on most wagons…mould seams.

On these examples, there is a prominent mould seam across the buffer heads and buffer beam which is unattractive and rather ruins the look of the model.

I remove these by scraping off with a hobby knife and, if necessary, rubbing with wet & dry paper to finish.

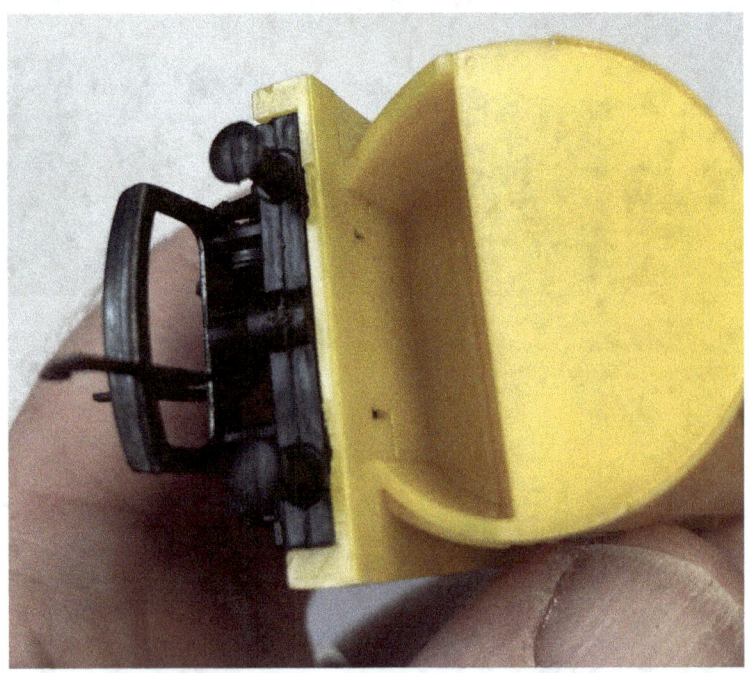

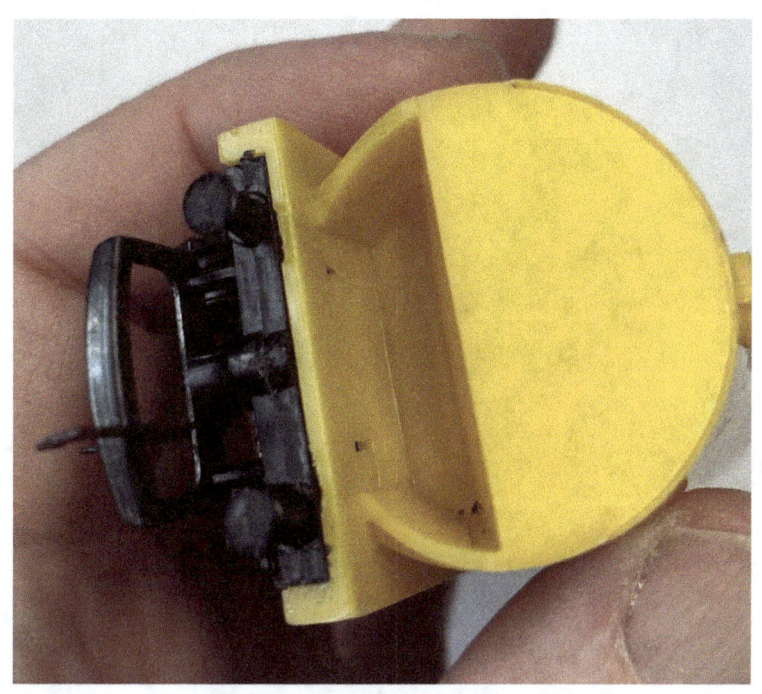

**Step 4**

Our attention can then turn to priming the wagon using grey acrylic primer.

We will not be applying any pre-shade on this wagon as colour modulation will be employed later.

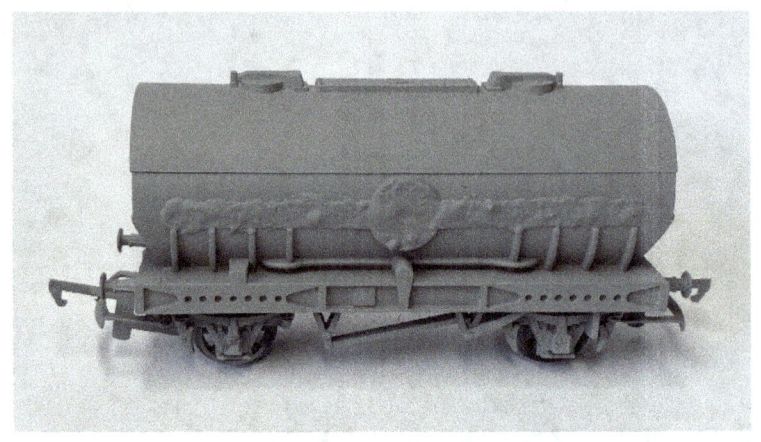

## Step 5

Once the primer is fully cured, the tanker body is airbrush painted with the darker yellow shade as the base colour.

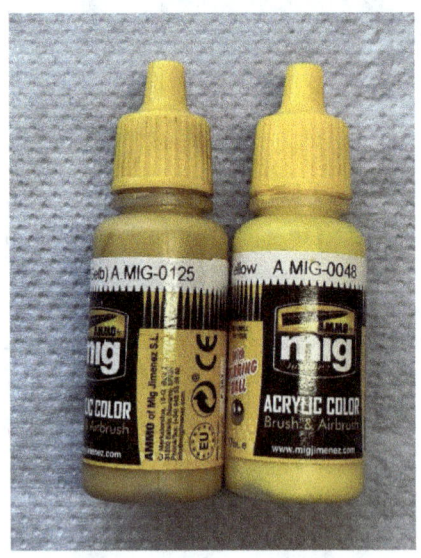

**Step 6**

Once the first yellow coat is dry, we will apply a fine coat of our lighter yellow taking care to just spray the middle sections of panels to provide colour modulation across the body side. A soft edge to the sprayed area provides a gentle graduation in the colour across the panels.

The effect is quite subtle and does not show up particularly well in photographs but gives a less monotone appearance to the paintwork.

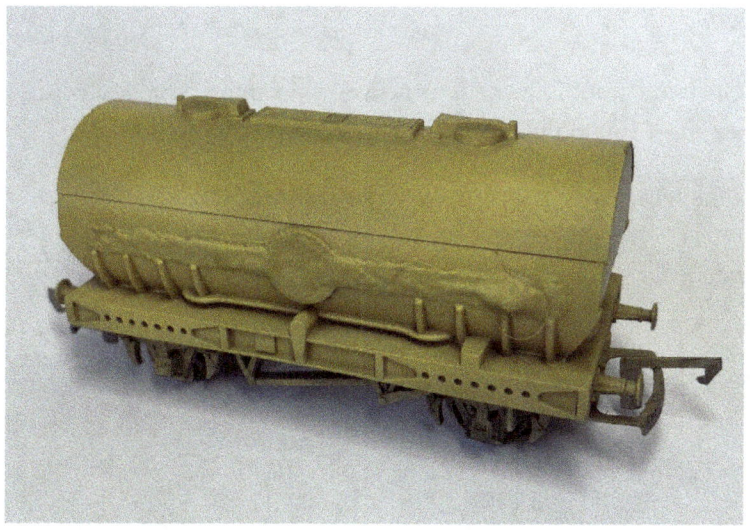

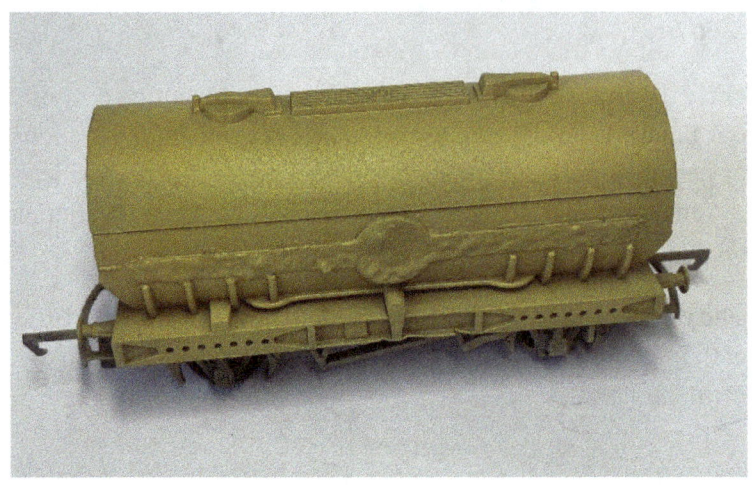

**Step 7**

Once the paint is fully dry, the Maskol can be removed using a pair of fine pointed tweezers.

This where you will find out if your Maskol application was neat or as messy as mine (and how much touching up is needed).

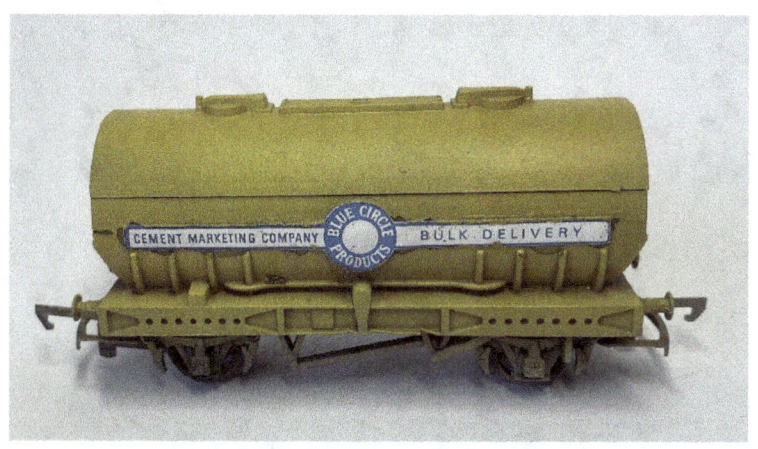

## Step 8

Using a 10/0 brush, touch up any areas where the Maskol has removed the base colour and allow to dry.

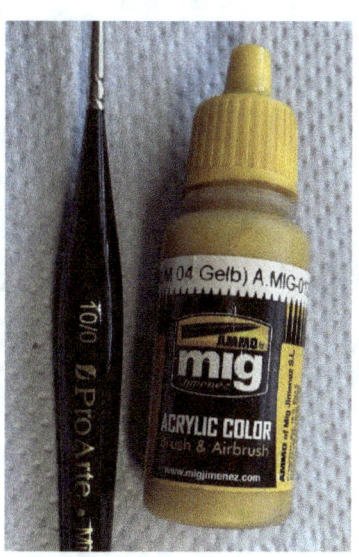

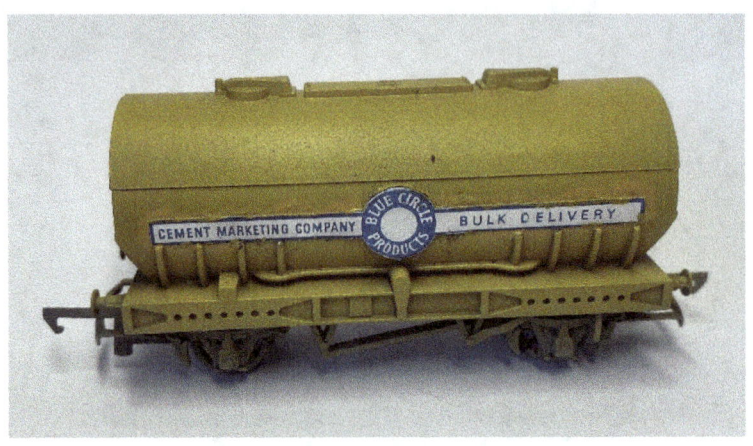

## Step 9

Using a 2/0 brush, the undercarriage can now be painted matt black.

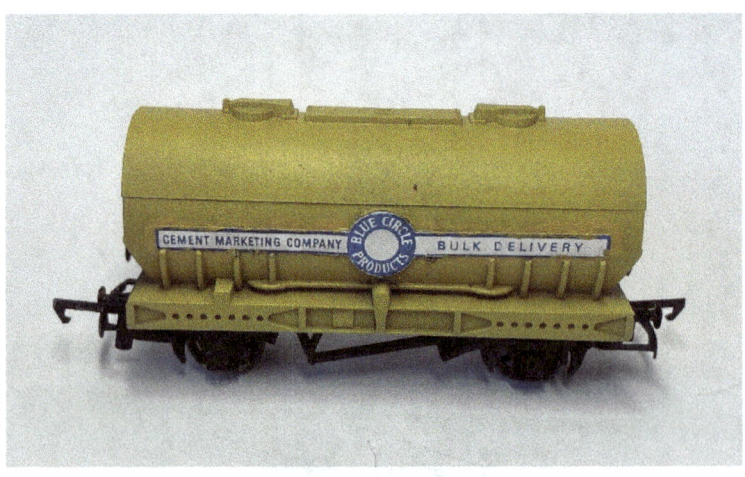

## Step 10

The wheels, brake shoes and leaf springs are then painted in our rust colour acrylic.

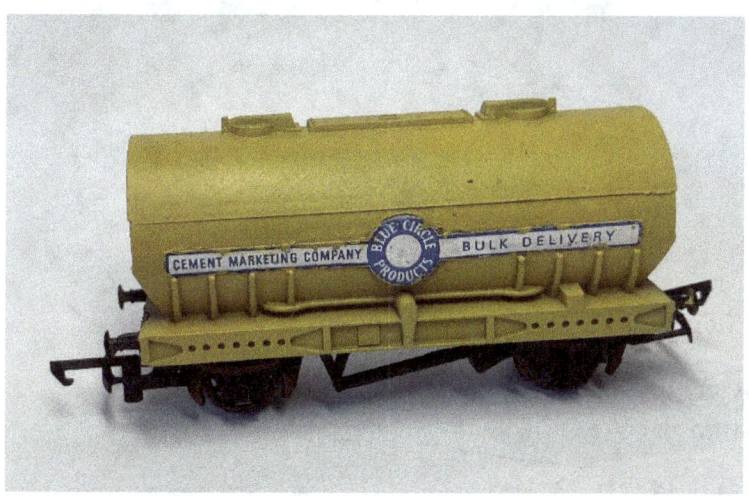

## Step 11

Using a small sponge piece held in tweezers, I then applied some very fine paint chips to the chassis rails and walkway using the rust colour acrylic (not strictly accurate due to the use of aluminium in the real thing but adds to the later effect).

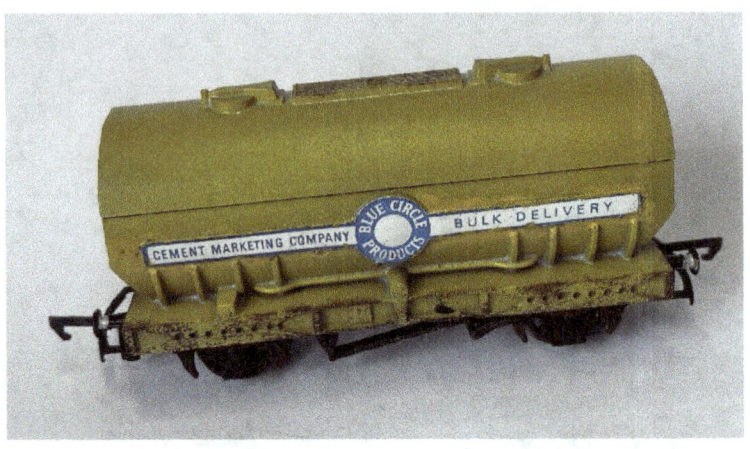

**Step 12**

Once dry, the wagon is airbrush coated with satin acrylic
varnish and allowed to fully cure.

**Step 13**

The next step will use the Light Dust Nature Effect as a wash
medium.

Shake the bottle well and stir the contents at the bottom of the
bottle before shaking it again as this type of liquid pigment
tends to settle.

First apply the effect around the chassis details and pipework
as a conventional wash.

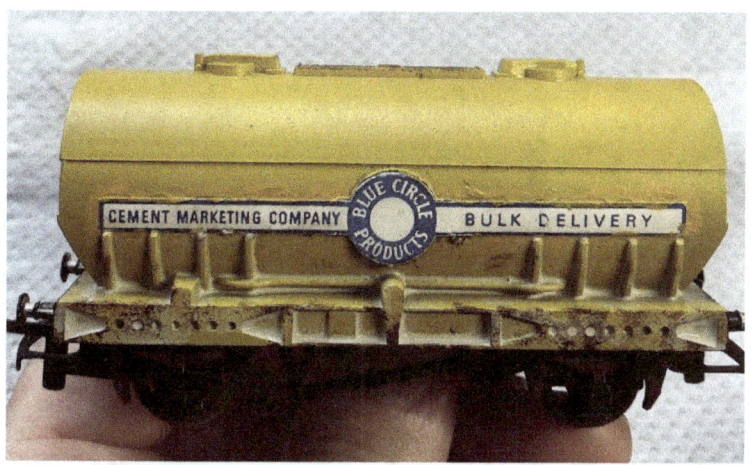

Then repeat for the detail on the tanker top.

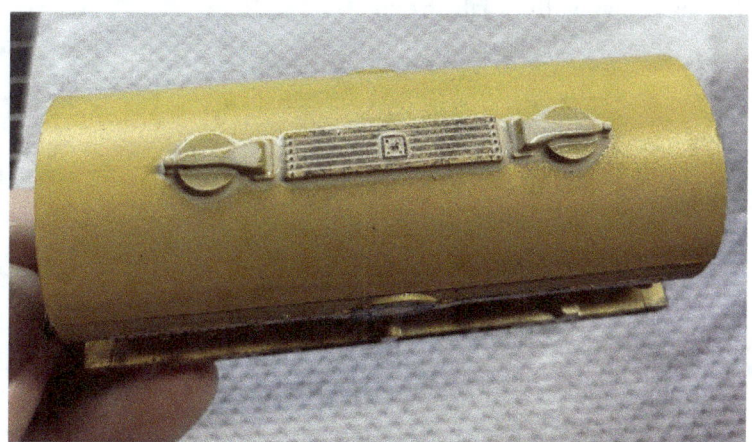

Finally, apply in the areas where streaking and deposits are required.

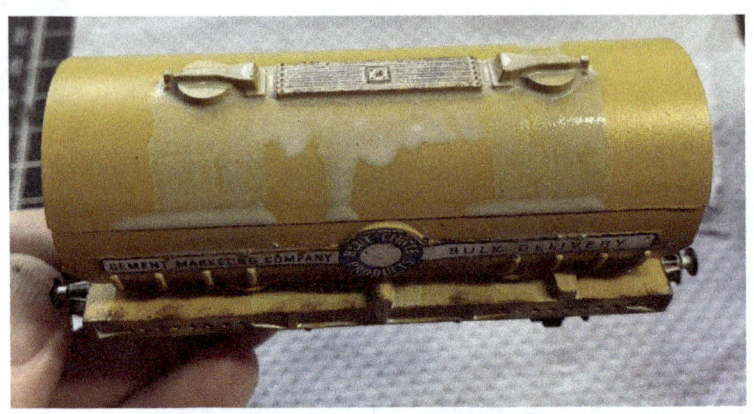

**Step 14**

Using a size 1 brush, form the wash into suitable streaks using vertical downward brush strokes.

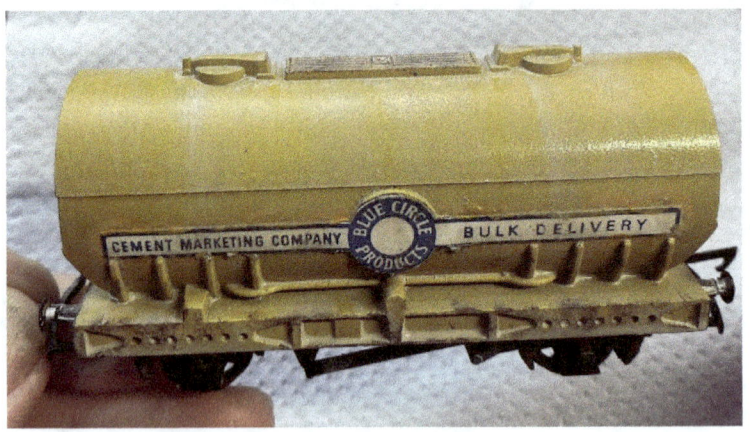

184

**Step 15**

Intensify the streaks below the filling hatches using further Nature Effect, I used the slightly thicker deposit from inside the lid for these areas.

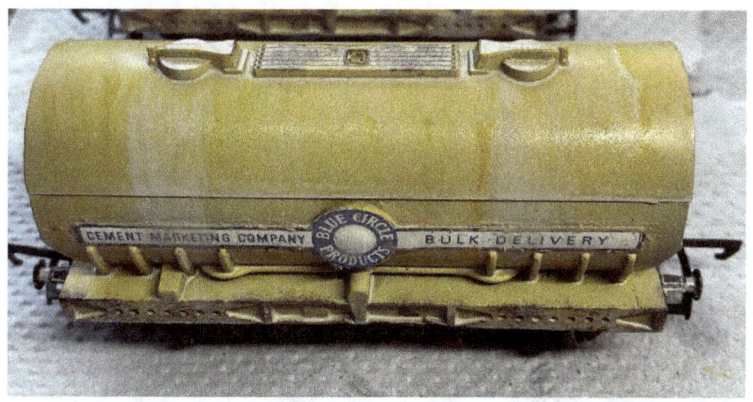

Allow to dry for 24 hours.

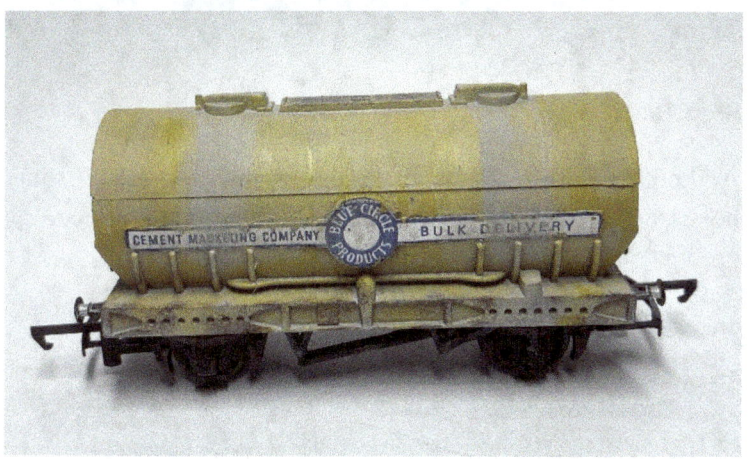

**Step 16**

Use the airbrush to apply a misted coat of our chosen dirt colour to the chassis and lower regions of the wagon body and body ends.

**Step 17**

Apply two coats of matt acrylic varnish using the airbrush.

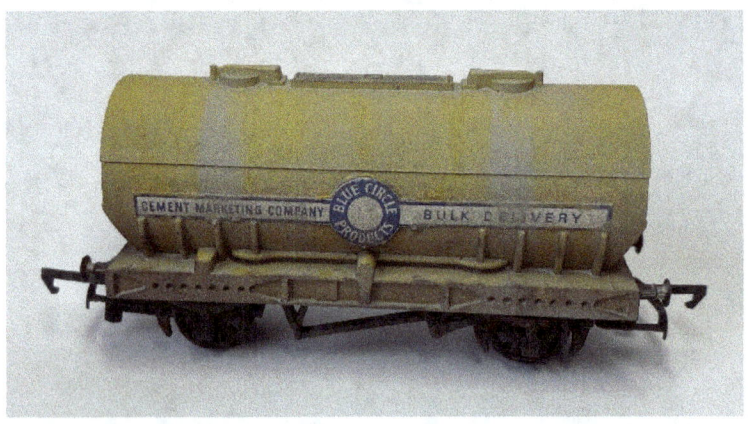

**Step 18**

Add oil and grease effects on the buffer ends and axle bearing boxes, applied using a 5/0 brush and our chosen oil effect product.

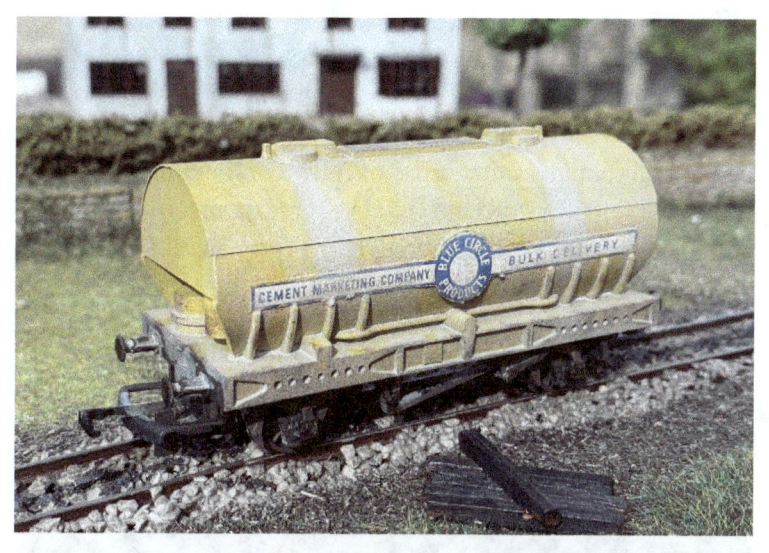

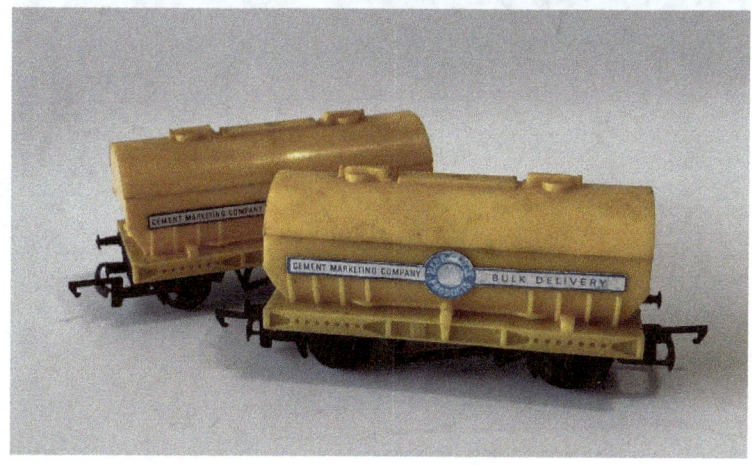

187

# Conclusion

Having worked through the projects in this book, you should now have a toolbox of painting and weathering skills that can be applied to many other areas of railway modelling. The best way to develop these skills is to use them as much as possible and to experiment with different techniques and different products.

It is not just rolling stock that can benefit from application of these techniques....

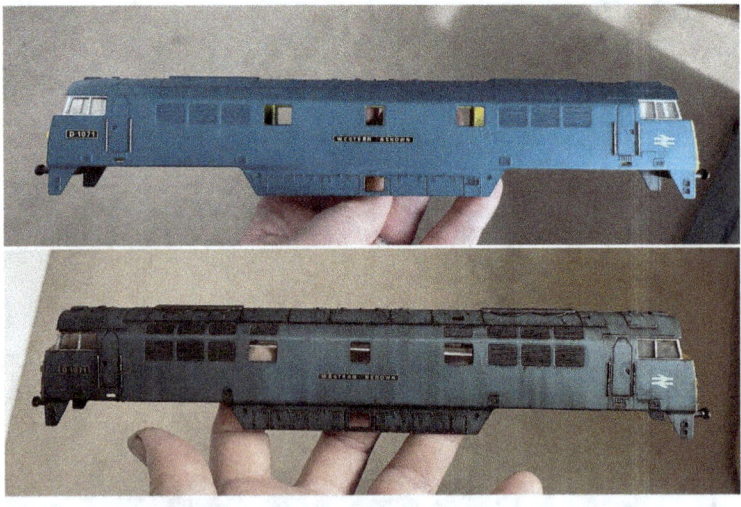

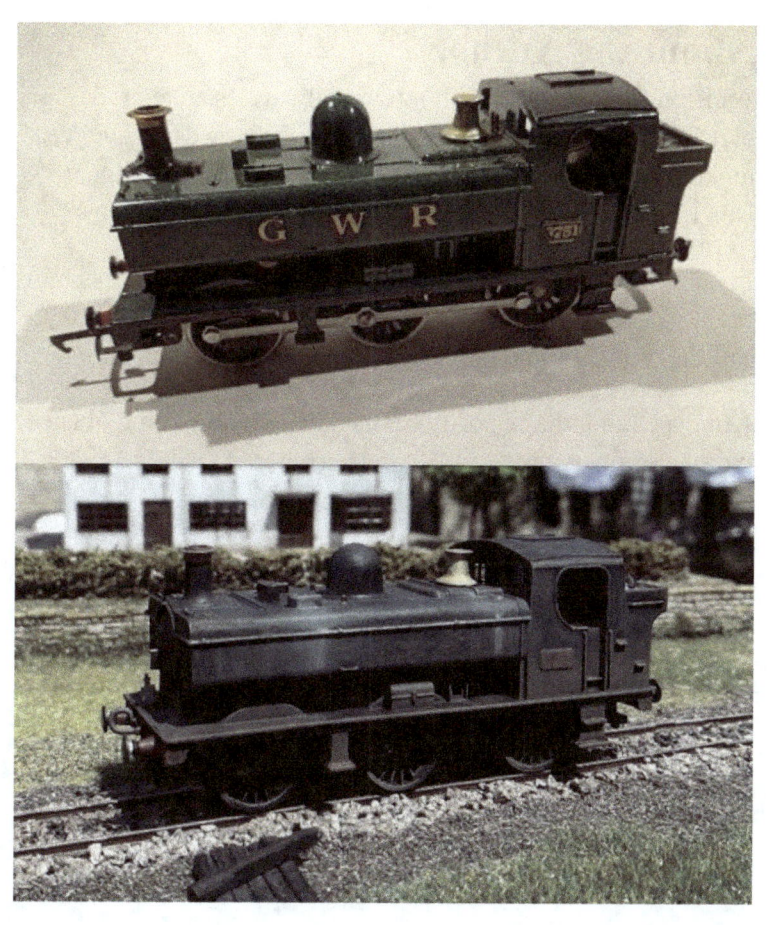

# About the Author

Winston Guy grew up with model railways as an everyday part of life in the 1970s and 1980s, his father was an avid OO modeller who, for a number of years, worked in the Signal Box model railway shop in Plymouth.

In later life, Winston returned to N gauge model railways but rapidly decided that model making, and the weathering aspects of railway models were his real interest in the hobby.

After spending the majority of his model making time over the succeeding years on 1/72 scale armoured vehicle models, Winston started to repaint and weather occasional OO railway models for sale on eBay.

By the time of publication, he had sold over 700 weathered railway models of various types and continues to try to bring interesting and unusual models to the world.

www.ingramcontent.com/pod-product-compliance
Lightning Source LLC
Chambersburg PA
CBHW070632220526
45466CB00001B/159